A Life to Remember

A Life to Remember

The Inspirational Story of Morella Kayman,
co-founder of the Alzheimer's Society

MORELLA KAYMAN

WITH NICOLE CARMICHAEL

JOHN BLAKE

Published by John Blake Publishing Ltd,
3 Bramber Court, 2 Bramber Road,
London W14 9PB, England

www.johnblakepublishing.co.uk

www.facebook.com/Johnblakepub 🟦
twitter.com/johnblakepub 🟦

First published in hardback in 2014

ISBN: 978-1-78219-988-5

British Library Cataloguing-in-Publication Data:

A catalogue record for this book is available from the British Library.

Design by www.envydesign.co.uk

Printed in Great Britain by CPI Group (UK) Ltd

1 3 5 7 9 10 8 6 4 2

© Text copyright Morella Kayman 2014

The right of Morella Kayman to be identified as the author of this
work has been asserted by her in accordance with the Copyright, Designs
and Patents Act 1988.

Papers used ⬚⬚⬚⬚⬚⬚⬚⬚⬚⬚⬚⬚⬚⬚⬚ natural, recyclable products made from
wood gro⬚⬚⬚⬚⬚⬚⬚⬚⬚⬚⬚⬚ The manufacturing processes conform to
⬚⬚⬚⬚⬚⬚⬚ environmental regulations of the country of origin.

Every attempt has been made to contact the relevant copyright-holders,
but some were unobtainable. We would be grateful if the appropriate people could
contact us.

Dedicated to the memory of Lawrence Fisher

CONTENTS

CONTENTS

FOREWORD

Fiona Phillips, Alzheimer's Society Ambassador

I can vividly remember meeting Morella Kayman for the first time. It was at a Parliamentary reception for supporters of Alzheimer's Society. I can't recall whether it was the House of Lords or Commons, or how I got there, or whether it was summer or winter, but I remember the exact moment I was introduced to Morella and where we were standing in the crowded room at the time. I can't picture much about the room either, come to that, but my first impression of Morella is firmly imprinted on my memory. A small, effervescent, very warm and glamorous bundle of energy, I immediately felt as though I already knew her. We spontaneously hugged each other, aware that between us was the unspoken knowledge that Alzheimer's had visited both of us and left its indelible mark.

I don't know what I had been expecting when I was told that I was going to be introduced to the co-founder of Alzheimer's Society, but I do recall being somewhat relieved and delighted that, despite the reverence in which she is held, Morella's approachability was a welcome surprise and confirmation of what I hoped she'd be. I can also recall thanking her for what she'd done.

I won't tell you too much about Morella's story; she can best do that in the following pages, but I do know that she knew very little about Alzheimer's disease when her beloved husband, Lawrence Fisher, was diagnosed in 1972.

If Morella didn't know much about it then, she didn't learn much from her pretty much unfruitful searches for help and information either. Her frustration was boundless when she found that very little seemed to be known about the condition, mainly because there was a taboo associated with it and therefore a veil of secrecy over it. It was considered a rather embarrassing, distressing part of ageing, best covered up and got on with. She struggled to find support and advice, but, nevertheless, battled on, caring for her husband, having recovered from cancer, alongside bringing up her young daughter. Despite this onerous burden of responsibility, or probably, because of it, she managed to dedicate what little time she had left to work at starting an organisation to support those affected by dementia.

As I said, I will leave the telling of that to Morella, but here's where I come in and why this remarkable lady means so much to me. My mother, Amy, was an infectiously happy spirit, who saw the good in everyone. Everyone loved her, even my grumpy teenage friends. Of course, I was embarrassed that she was so warm, welcoming and friendly at the time – that's what teenagers do! But looking back on my childhood, I see a huge hug of my mother's love and recall her oft-repeated 'As long as you're happy, I'm happy' reassurance.

It was when she hit her mid- to late 50s that she changed. Even if I was happy, she was not. She often cried, did silly things, seemed uninterested in my two brothers and me, a change that was reflected in her eyes, which lost their twinkling sparkle. I lived in

London, she and my father lived in Wales, so, while I saw them as often as I could, I didn't know what was going on from day to day.

There was something different about Mum's manner on the phone, though, and I got irritated, thinking she didn't care about me like she used to. When I travelled to Wales, I could see that relations between Mum and Dad were more than strained, but I put that down to the normal ins and outs of a long marriage. I'll scoot over the years, because it wasn't until she was 62, and spent a whole week on her own with me, that I could see she was more than depressed. I kept reassuring her that her doctor would sort things out.

The next time I spent time on my own with her was when I had my first son. She came to stay, to help. I was devastated to find out that it was she who needed help. She didn't know how to turn the kettle on, was confused by the kitchen taps, couldn't operate the toaster, had difficulty counting money out in shops, had forgotten her bank card pin number, had involuntary facial movements, night terrors … the list is long. I found out she was on anti-depressants, so assumed she had clinical depression. I got in touch with her doctor and was told she was being referred for Alzheimer's disease. But that can't be right, I thought; that's all about older people who say funny things and there was nothing funny about what was happening to Mum. I didn't know what to do, so I turned to my computer and looked it up. Up popped the Alzheimer's Society website, which gave me a huge sense of relief. It made me feel as though I wasn't alone and it armed me with information and facts to go forward. Mum was 67 when we finally realised what was wrong with her.

She died in 2006 aged 74, after suffering alone for years. Throughout, my father hadn't been a great help at all. We found out why, when, just a couple of months after Mum's death, we found out that he had Alzheimer's too.

That is also a long story, but this is Morella Kayman's story. An account of how one remarkable woman's battle for information about, and help with, Alzheimer's disease has ultimately meant so much to the hundreds of thousands of people and their families affected by this cruel disease. I am proud to be an ambassador for Alzheimer's Society. But I am more than proud to have been asked to introduce you to the lady whose refusal to be told to 'just get on with it' and whose determination to get something done about it has brought invaluable help and reassurance to so many.

What is Alzheimer's disease?
(© alzheimers.org.uk)
Alzheimer's disease is the most common cause of dementia, affecting around 496,000 people in the UK. The term 'dementia' describes a set of symptoms which can include loss of memory, mood changes, and problems with communication and reasoning. These symptoms occur when the brain is damaged by certain diseases and conditions, including Alzheimer's disease.

Alzheimer's disease, first described by the German neurologist Alois Alzheimer, is a physical disease affecting the brain. During the course of the disease, protein 'plaques' and 'tangles' develop in the structure of the brain, leading to the death of brain cells. People with Alzheimer's also have a shortage of some important chemicals in their brain. These chemicals are involved with the transmission of messages within the brain.

Alzheimer's is a progressive disease, which means that gradually, over time, more parts of the brain are damaged. As this happens, the symptoms become more severe.

INTRODUCTION:

Thursday, 16 February 2012

It felt like I was dreaming. As our car pulled up to the gates of Buckingham Palace, I squeezed my daughter Mandy's hand and took a deep breath. Like so many people, I had often stood at these magnificent gates before, hoping that I might catch a glimpse of the Queen inside. As a child, I had hoped that she might spot me and give me a little wave; if only I had known then that one day I would be travelling through these gates as an officially invited guest …

That day in February 2012, I had been up since the early hours of the morning, unable to sleep through a mixture of worry and excitement about what lay ahead. In the car with Mandy and me were my two grandchildren, Katie and Oliver, and my sister Angela.

During the hour's drive to Buckingham Palace from our homes in north London, we chatted excitedly about what was going to happen and whether we might see any celebrities. Katie and Oliver joked about how terrible it would be if I tripped as I was being presented to the Queen to receive my MBE, and I laughed nervously. I didn't want to tempt fate, but secretly it had been worrying me, too.

We arrived at 10.10am at the South Centre Gate entrance to Buckingham Palace, where our passes were checked and we were shown where to park. It was a gorgeous bright crisp morning and everyone was so happy and welcoming. It was such a celebratory atmosphere.

We were ushered inside the Palace and I was instructed to go up one side of a staircase, while Mandy and co went up the other side to the Ballroom, where the ceremony was going to take place. Suddenly, I felt very alone and started getting very nervous. I have looked back at footage from that day and, while it may look as if I am smiling, it is really more of a grimace. Truth be told, I was absolutely terrified!

Some 94 people were due to be invested that day, including five new knights, and there were a further 300 or so family and friends there to support everyone. Usually you are allowed up to three guests, but I had begged to be allowed to bring an extra guest. My daughter, sister and grandchildren are the most important people in my life and I would have found it impossible to exclude one of them. I have no idea what I would have done if they had insisted that I bring only three people with me.

Although receiving an honour from the Queen is obviously a very formal occasion, everyone was so warm and friendly, and they all genuinely seemed to want to make the occasion feel special. Everybody was dressed so smartly and yet it didn't feel intimidating at all. Lieutenant Colonel Andrew Ford, in his role as Controller of the Lord Chamberlain's Office, presided over the day's events. He went out of his way to put us at our ease and made sure we all knew what was going to happen, telling us where we were expected to stand and explaining to us the etiquette of how to address the

Queen – 'Your Majesty' the first time, then 'Ma'am' every time after that, and so on.

Some 26 investitures are held every year and each event is choreographed with the utmost precision. Sometimes it is the Queen who hands out the honours, at other times it can be Prince Philip, Princess Anne or another member of the royal family. Today, however, I was to receive my MBE from the Queen, which I was thrilled about. Not that I have anything against the rest of the royal family, of course, it was just such an honour to be face to face with Her Majesty.

When the investiture is held at Buckingham Palace, as the guests gather in the Ballroom, the people who are about to receive their awards are briefed beforehand in the beautiful John Nash Picture Gallery. I spotted Ronnie Corbett – who was going to receive a CBE that day – chatting and laughing in a circle of people, which included the golfer Lee Westwood, but I was far too nervous to go and introduce myself.

I was instructed where to wait before my name was called out and then told where to stand as the Queen pinned on my MBE. It was explained to me that, when the Queen shakes your hand, it is the signal that she has finished talking to you and that you are to take a few steps backwards – preferably without falling over! – and then rejoin your family and friends.

I tried to stay as calm as possible and to take in every detail as my name was read out – 'Mrs Kayman, Morella, for services to the Alzheimer's Society' – and then I made my way towards the Queen. I didn't expect Her Majesty to say anything more than perhaps a simple hello or congratulations, and so I was a little taken aback when she said: 'You hear so much more about Alzheimer's these days, don't you? And, of course, you don't need to be old to be affected by it.' I agreed and mentioned to her that my husband Lawrence had been relatively young when he was diagnosed. I felt that we chatted for quite a time before she shook my hand. What a moment! I then stepped back – without falling over (hurrah!) – and went and joined Mandy, Angela, Katie and Oliver, who were all beaming with pride. We all wanted to whoop with joy, but we had to contain ourselves.

For all of us, life is a mixture of joy and sorrow. As the old proverb says, the person who has never tasted what is bitter does not know what is sweet. There have certainly been occasions when I have felt as if I have had more than my fair share of tears, but I have had plenty of wonderful, joyful times, too – including, of course, that special day when I received my MBE, which I now consider to be one of the proudest of my life. Through good and bad, I have so many extraordinary memories I would like to share with my friends and family, and I hope that what follows is a true and accurate account of my life, and of the people who have shaped it ...

CHAPTER 1

My darling mother Binnie had a very interesting story to tell, not least because of the 'family scandal' that brought her and my father together in the late 1920s. Growing up, though, I knew hardly anything about her childhood, other than the fact that she had been born on 16 February 1907 in Lodz in Central Poland and moved to England in the early 1920s when she was a teenager. When the Second World War ended in 1945, she had tried to find out from the authorities what had happened to the rest of her family, but it was to no avail. When none of them could be tracked down, she came to accept that they had in all likelihood perished in the Holocaust, although some years later she was reunited with her sister Rosa. Even though she did finally meet Rosa again, I feel sure that she carried a kind of survivor's guilt with her throughout her life, and suspect it was for that reason that she didn't tell me more about her early family history – it was as if she wanted to blank it out from the past.

As I have gone through my life and terrible things have

happened, I too have learned how to blank things out of my past. Sometimes memories are too haunting to bear.

Binnie's father's name was Aaron Moszek. She never told us the details of what she had to go through in her childhood, but I could always sense that things were often hard for her and her siblings, and I gathered that she never had any formal education. It was for this reason, I think, that she was so determined that Angela and I should work hard and try to better ourselves in any way that we could. She was always trying to educate herself and behave in a way that she felt would befit the wife of a businessman, which of course she went on to become once she married my father. She left her history behind when she stepped off that boat from Poland and refused to speak about it for many years. I know it seems strange now, but growing up I never really gave it a second thought. It was just the way we were brought up, and that was that.

My father Phillip was born in Warsaw in 1890, the fifth child of Rose and Morris Pfeffer, who died in 1934 and 1944 respectively. My grandparents emigrated to England in 1906, and anglicised their name to Pepperman soon after they arrived. My father's sister, Esther-Beila, meanwhile, married a man called Woolf Goodkind, who had also come to England from Russia in 1904 and went into the business of manufacturing furs under the name of W Goodkind & Sons.

My father, meanwhile, traded in fur skins and set up his own very successful furrier business in his twenties. Apart from the obvious family connection, I don't know why my father chose this particular field; I imagine he thought it might provide him with a good standard of living – which, indeed, it did – and, like my mother, he was also always very keen to better himself. He went into partnership with his brother, Abraham Levy, who was the second eldest in the family, and they called their business Levy Pepperman and had premises in the City of London.

Quite why my father was a Pepperman and Abraham was a Levy has always been something of a mystery. We never really got to the bottom of why they had different surnames – again, that was just the way it was – and, strange as it may seem, we never really questioned it. As I came to discover in later life, there were all sorts of anomalies in my childhood. If I were in similar situations now, I would say, 'Hang on, why did that happen?' But at the time, you just go with the flow. What I do know, though, is that back then a lot of Jewish immigrants from Poland wanted to assimilate as much as possible and, to that end, many adopted anglicised names. I have no idea why my uncle had decided that he wanted to be known as a Levy – it could, I suppose, be that he just preferred the name to Pepperman. (After all, Pepperman, as I was later to discover, was a great name to make fun of. When I was a little girl at school, one of my nicknames was Pepperpot as I was quite stubby and round.)

Dad was a good and generous man. I remember him as being bald and quite short, and having the most wonderful smiley face, though as a younger man he had lots of dark hair. Looking back at old photos, he always looks as if he is just about to break into a smile. I always thought he was very handsome, and he was loved and respected by everybody.

For that reason, it came as quite a shock to me when, in my early twenties, I learned about the terrible family scandal that had brought my parents together. A so-called dear friend of my father told me, clearly not thinking about how devastated I would be by what I heard.

At the time, I was working for my father and, whenever the opportunity arose, I would join him and his cronies for lunch at the Bonbonniere Restaurant in Woodstock Street, just off Oxford Street in central London, where he worked. One day, however, I went without my father and it was then that his so-called friend decided that he would put the record straight about how my parents began their relationship.

Apropos of absolutely nothing, he informed me that my father had previously been married to my mother's aunt, Becky. I was aghast. I don't know why he decided at that moment to tell me. Maybe he found it odd that even in my twenties I was still a real Daddy's girl and he wanted to show me how that the fine upstanding Mr Pepperman was actually harbouring a dark secret.

I was very confused and upset by what I had been told and found it difficult to believe; the fact that my dear father had married his niece sounded like some kind of incest to me. It just didn't make sense. The moment I got home, I asked him if there was any truth to the story, desperately hoping that he would deny it.

But, of course, he couldn't. He explained to me that he had married Becky when he was very young and that, for all intents and purposes, it was an arranged marriage; their parents had decided that Becky and Phillip would make a good pairing whether they liked it or not. He and Becky had tried hard to make the marriage work, but they never had children, which is something that my father had always desperately wanted. As a result, he said, their relationship was quite strained and, with time, as it became plain that they were never going to have children together, they accepted that the marriage was doomed. Back then, for people like my father, if you were married, you had children, simple as that.

Meanwhile, in the 1920s and 1930s, Jews in Poland feared for their lives. Many wanted to flee, but this was difficult for them to do without assistance from outside the country. Somehow, my father had become involved in helping to get Jews out of Poland. It wasn't something he ever talked about at the time. I don't for a moment imagine it could have been 100 per cent legal and so it certainly wasn't the sort of thing that you would talk about in public. It was an incredibly difficult time for the Jews in Poland and my father was determined to do anything he could to help, and if that meant cutting a few corners, then so be it. Anti-Semitism was rife and, even though Britain was seen as a safe haven, my father did not broadcast the fact that he was involved in aiding the passage of Jews into the country.

One such refugee that my father helped was Becky's teenage niece, Binnie – my mother. She was 20 years younger than him, very beautiful, with long dark hair and clear sparkly eyes. When she arrived in London, it was love at first sight for both of them. They knew it would tear the family apart if they were ever to give in to their feelings, but they couldn't help themselves. They had to be together. My father knew that such a relationship would be a terrible scandal and greatly upsetting to all of the family, but they were so in love with one another and, as he tried to explain to me, it wasn't as if they were actually blood relatives.

My father's marriage was over in all but name by this stage, and it was not long after Binnie's arrival that he left Becky to be with her. They had the most wonderful relationship together from that day onwards and went on to have two daughters – my sister Angela, who was born in 1930, and me, in 1934. My father was still married to Becky when we were born, but they subsequently divorced, and he and my mother married on 30 June 1943 at the Marylebone Registry Office in London (a place that would feature in my life 43 years later). Neither Angela nor myself was at the wedding, which was witnessed by my father's best friends, Sam Green and Kingsley Clifford. For obvious reasons, it was all rather hush-hush.

My mother had previously changed her name by deed poll to Pepperman, so, when I was born, her name showed up as Pepperman on my birth certificate. So, if I hadn't been told about 'the family scandal' that fateful day at the Bonbonniere, I may never have been aware of it.

CHAPTER 2

We were a happy family in the main. I remember that my parents seemed to argue quite a bit, but, then again, they had a very passionate relationship and my mother could be very excitable, so maybe it was just natural for her to raise her voice from time to time. She had a very strong personality and certainly wasn't everybody's cup of tea; she was very much a love-her-or-loathe-her character. For my part, though, I always adored my mother and she was always very affectionate with me. She could also be quite formidable and strict – in those days, a slap or two was acceptable punishment and I certainly got my full share, even for things I hadn't necessarily done! That said, the day when I tripped up at home and proceeded to smash an entire eight-piece Limoges dinner service I don't remember being punished for it, so she couldn't have been that bad. Writing it down here, it all sounds terribly tempestuous, but, for all the quarrels and quibbles, there was also an awful lot of love.

My mother didn't always understand my needs and foibles as I was growing up, in part, I suppose, because we had been brought up in such different environments. The world was moving forward so quickly. My father had been born in the previous century and my mother grew up before women even had the right to vote. Meanwhile, I think I was determined to be independent practically from the day I was born!

We lived in a lovely house in Southgate in north London until the outbreak of war in 1939, at which point we moved up to Lancashire. By then, my father was very well known in the fur trade and, while not a religious Jew, was a committed Zionist. He later bought land and orange groves when the state of Israel was established in 1948. He was a great supporter of Israel and also supported many charities at home.

Before the war, my father's business was based in the City, but afterwards he got larger premises in Oxford Street, opposite Selfridges. It was from there that we watched many amazing royal processions, including Queen Elizabeth's Coronation in 1953, when he invited so many people to his showroom to join us that we were bursting at the seams! I remember he hired tiered seating so that everyone would have a good view from his showroom windows. If only I had known then that one day I would actually meet her.

Growing up, we had quite a sizeable extended family. My father was particularly close to his eldest sister, Esther-Beila Goodkind (who was known as Beila), and her six sons who all called him Uncle Pep. I don't recall what the age difference was between my father and Beila, but as she was the eldest and my father was the youngest, she would have been old enough to be my grandma, and I suppose I saw her in that role. The last of her sons to get married was Sydney, her second eldest, who married a wonderful woman called Phyllis. Aunt Beila eventually went to live with them in Hampstead after Woolf died.

Beila became known as 'Grandma Goodkind' to absolutely everyone and for many years we spent most Friday nights and many of the Jewish holidays together at Phyllis and Sydney's house with the whole family. Friday nights are always very special in Jewish households as they are the time when the whole family comes together for prayers and supper.

During the First World War, Woolf Goodkind took his six sons and extended family, including my father, Uncle Pep, out of London and rented a house in the lovely village of Woburn Sands, not far from what is now Milton Keynes; it was big enough for the whole family to visit. Then, during the Second World War, Woolf rented another house in Woburn Sands and relocated his business to Bedfordshire as, like my father, he wanted to get out of London during the war. He managed to get a government contract making sheepskin flying jackets and helmets for pilots and aircrew. My father supplied the sheepskin and the Goodkinds manufactured the garments.

(I was recently reminded that when I was about eight I was often to be found hiding in the bales of skins when playing hide and seek with Daddy!)

It was never a quiet time on those occasions as there was always quite a number of us. Lots of children, lots of noise. Phyllis and Sydney had twin sons Wallace and Michael, who were always playing pranks and pretending they were the other one. Whenever they got the opportunity – not when we were having Friday night dinner, of course! – they would swap identities. I remember one time when they were teenagers they took the same girl to the cinema. One sat with her during the first part of the film and then they swapped around at the interval. Maybe she secretly knew, maybe she didn't, but she certainly never acted as if she had rumbled their plan. A week later, both boys developed chicken pox, which she had been recovering from at the time but just neglected to tell them. Maybe she had the last laugh, after all.

I also remember Wallace and Michael playing football in the garden with 'Grandma Goodkind' in goal. It is a picture I will never forget as they hoofed the ball towards her and she had to try to make a save – such good times and so many laughs. Tragically, both brothers died of heart attacks when they were relatively young: Wallace was 44 and Michael was in his mid-fifties.

My grandfather on my father's side had died before I was born and, when war broke out, my grandmother – Booba, as we called her – went to live in the country, safe from the bombs. She was a very strict orthodox Jew and my strongest memory of her is seeing her lying in a great big four-poster bed with one of her many sheitels (wigs) strewn over one of the bedposts. She lived in a lovely house and the whole family would visit whenever we could. I never really knew her, but, to the best of my memory, she did not speak any English, only Polish or Yiddish, and so it was difficult for me to think of her as my grandma as we could not communicate. Apparently, she was also quite a dominant woman, as I think so many women were at the time.

My sister Angela and I had a terrible relationship when we were younger and used to fight like cat and dog. We were very competitive, as so many siblings are, and I used to think she was a bit jealous of how close I was to Mummy. We were always quite different; I loved showing off and singing, whereas she was always very good at drawing and other creative things. She also had the most wonderful thick hair and Mummy would put it into ringlets for her, while mine was really fine and tangled and I would howl and howl whenever I had to have it brushed. Angela was also much cleverer with words than I was; if we ever had cross words (which was quite often) she would always win the argument with a clever put-down. Now, of course, I know it was just part and parcel of growing up, but at the time it felt like torture. So frustrating!

I was always very close to my father. He was a great card player and throughout my childhood he tried to teach me various games, such as gin rummy and kalooki. Incredibly, whenever I played gin rummy with him, I somehow managed to beat him – on reflection, though, I think Dad was just being his usual generous self and letting me win. As I got older and eventually started to learn bridge, I told my father how bad I was at it and he told me in no uncertain terms that I must never show my opponents that I thought I wasn't as good as they were. It was good advice. I have bluffed my way to many a victory ever since.

Colourful family memories and snapshots of happy times like my cousins in goal with Grandma Goodkind form lovely memories, but as a child I didn't think about the whys or wherefores of family events. As with so many other people's childhoods, you just live it at the time and take it for granted. For me, everything just merges into a cherished blanket of warm memories.

I will always remember it as a very happy time with all of us playing together, celebrating holidays and surrounded by the love of my extended family. I had a wonderfully secure life. We weren't exactly rich and driving around in fancy cars, but we were certainly very comfortable, and I feel blessed that my father was able to provide so well for us. My mother would often remind us how lucky we were and repeatedly told us that we should always try to help and support people less fortunate than ourselves. This was instilled in us from a very young age; there was never any question that we would do anything else. If you have enough money, you should share it.

CHAPTER 3

When the Second World War began, my sister was nine and I was five. I was too young to understand what was going on around me, but I knew that all of a sudden there seemed to be a lot of fuss, with lots of people coming over to the house, plans being made and so on.

My father evacuated the whole family to St Anne's-on-Sea in Lancashire. He was too old to sign up – by then, he was 49 and my mother was 29. Dad had always dedicated himself to protecting the family and so there was never any question that we would stay in London. Besides, he saw an opportunity to set up a new business in Manchester, and so off we went. My sister and I went to primary school there and we quickly started to make friends in the way that young children always seem to be able to do wherever they go. If only it was so easy now, I'm sure the world would be a better place.

My parents rented a house in St Andrew's Road North, opposite the railway line in St Anne's. It wasn't a big house, but we were very happy there. We had a dog and a cat, and there was a yard at the back where we rode our bicycles, and of course an outside toilet, though that wasn't the slightest bit unusual at the time.

I have fond memories of my father coming home from work and listening to the radio, every hour on the hour, when the news was on. These were the days before the average person could even consider having a television set and, anyway, television broadcasting was suspended from September 1939 until June 1946. The radio was essential to everyone and became a focal point for families. Just like in those old television movies you see, we really did all sit around the wireless listening to the news.

As it was for everyone, food rationing was a major challenge of daily life. I have difficulty remembering much detail about it because I was so young at the time, but I do know that my favourite meal in those days was carrots and potato all mashed up with butter – if we could get the real thing, that is. To have meat or fish was a real luxury as fresh food was so scarce in those days. I used to queue up with my mother outside the local shops to spend the coupons that we were issued with on luxuries. To have a cake made with real eggs and butter was an almost unbelievable treat.

Mummy was very traditional and somehow she was able to create great meals. Many of her friends from back home in London had children who were soldiers, sailors and air force men that had been billeted in or near St Anne's, and they would often come to our house for Sunday lunch along with their friends. It was a lovely 'normal' day for them as they could set aside the war for a while and just feel they were visiting family for lunch. For that reason, Sundays were always the highlight of my week. I have always enjoyed big family meals with everyone around the table, laughing and chatting.

Perhaps because of her very own humble background, Mummy was very good at making absolutely the best out of anything she had to cook. She was the only person I have ever known who was able to make chicken soup out of an old boiler chicken, then roast the same chicken and serve it up for another meal. Normally, the chickens that are used for chicken soup are too old to be used for anything other than soup, but Mummy managed to maximise every meal. People would come from far and wide for her sweet and sour fish and her soups and stews always had lots of delicious spices. She was one of those people who never have to use a recipe book as she was a completely intuitive cook. For years, she used to cook on a tiny Belling cooker – goodness knows how she managed. I guess – unlike me, I'm afraid to say – she just had a real talent.

(Oh, if only I had inherited that gift! I'm not a bad cook, just a plain cook. I'm always worried that a recipe won't turn out the way it is meant to, but I haven't given anyone food poisoning – yet.)

CHAPTER 4

One of my most vivid memories of that time in St Anne's was the wonderful swimming pool that we used to go to at school. I was considered quite a good swimmer, and I remember being really proud that, unlike most of the other children, I was allowed to dive in at the deep end. I felt really quite special and I used to go as often as I could.

I also went to Brownies, then Guides, and I enjoyed horse riding, skating and dancing. Looking back on those years, it seems as if that all I did was go from one class to another; I really was very lucky and had a wonderful childhood. Funnily enough, I can't remember much about my first school and the academic side of things – I obviously decided then that it wasn't going to be a cherished memory – but I certainly remember all of the after-school activities.

There is one skating event, however, that was to have consequences for my entire life.

Although I say it myself, my skating was really good for my age

– so good, in fact, that at the tender age of seven I was invited to be in an ice show in Blackpool. I was desperate to do it. I was always a bit of a show-off when I was a child and I wasn't going to give up the opportunity of performing at a gala in front of a real live audience.

Unfortunately, on the day of the dress rehearsal, I woke up with swollen glands in my neck and my mother told me in no uncertain terms that I couldn't go. She said – quite sensibly, to be fair to her – that all the cold air wouldn't be good for me and that I should stay home and rest. I was heartbroken and I nagged and nagged and nagged, in the way that hysterical little girls often can, until I wore her down and she finally agreed that I could go.

If anything was ever to prove that mother knows best, this was it. I went along to the dress rehearsal, but the combination of over-exerting myself and the chill from the freezing cold ice rink meant that by the time I got home my glands were even more swollen and I was feeling very ill indeed. There was absolutely no way that I could disguise it either. My mother was at her wits' end with worry and, to make matters worse, she couldn't reach the doctor. She was cross with me, but really more cross with herself for not having been more strict about the situation. Finally, when she did manage to track down the doctor and speak to him, he told her that he wouldn't be able to come out and visit immediately, and instead instructed her to apply a hot poultice on my neck.

The doctor said to make sure that the poultice was as hot as I could possibly bear, as this would help bring the swelling down. Mummy duly prepared the poultice and tested the temperature, only then to realise that she had forgotten the cotton wool that she needed to apply it with. Once she retrieved the cotton wool, she then had to reheat the poultice, only this time she didn't test the temperature again before pressing it on to my poor neck …

As she put the heavy red-hot poultice on my neck and started tightly bandaging it up, I screamed and screamed as the heat seared through me. Trouble was, she thought I was just being a bit over-dramatic – I wonder why! – and carried on winding around the bandage. As far as she was concerned, she had tested the poultice the first time around and it had been fine, and so she had no reason to think it wouldn't be this time either. Finally, after I had been screaming and crying for about half an hour, she thought that it might be a good idea if she took it off after all, but I was in such a state that I wouldn't let her touch me. It was all too horrific.

By the time the doctor eventually arrived some three hours later, my neck was severely burned. Even the doctor winced when he saw it and he did his best to calm the pair of us down. My mother was mortified about what she had done to me and was in quite a state. The burn looked and felt terrible for several days after. It was so raw and blistered, and my neck looked ghastly, as if it had been chewed up by some kind of machine. The burn covered the whole area on the right side of my neck and, even though the pain eventually wore off, the scarring was really awful.

Unfortunately, even worse was to come. For the whole of the next year I had to go to Manchester three times a week to undergo deep x-ray treatment on the area to help flatten the skin and eradicate the scarring. At the time, of course, it was considered to be quite a revolutionary technique; cosmetic surgery, after all, wasn't as common or as advanced as it is today. But people didn't realise that that exposure to radiation could be dangerous and it would eventually prove to have a major effect on my future life.

Whatever pain I suffered that afternoon and in the years that followed as a result of all the x-ray treatment, nothing compared to the suffering my mother endured for the rest of her life, knowing that she had caused the accident to happen in the first place. Meanwhile, even though I was shocked to the core by the events, I continued to skate – though now only as a hobby, never anything more serious – and I tried to carry on all my other activities as normal. However ugly it was, I wasn't about to let anything like a silly burn stop me.

Through all this time, my father was his usual lovely self. He was of course very sad that I had to go through so much stress at such a young age with all of the x-ray treatments, but the good side to all this was that it meant I had to go to Manchester with him three times a week. It gave me the opportunity to spend more one-on-one time with him, which was wonderful; I absolutely adored him. We used to catch the train together and would chat all the way there and all the way back – suffice to say, between us, my father and I were never short of words. He would be so lovely with me after I had finished my treatment and always gave me lots of cuddles and fuss on the way home.

CHAPTER 5

Towards the end of the war, we all moved back to London and, soon after, Angela and I were sent to Ashford, a boarding school for girls in Kent. At the time, though, in common with many schools, pupils were relocated as a result of the war and, for our first year there, the school was based down in Exeter. From our second year onwards, we all returned to the original school in Kent.

I never really found out the reason why we were sent away to a boarding school rather than going to a regular day school in London, but at that age we didn't really question their decision. Actually, thinking about it, I don't think we ever questioned any of my parents' decisions – we wouldn't dare! I do remember, though, that Angela had nagged my parents to send us to a boarding school because she had loved the idea of the dormitories and getting up to all sorts of mischief. In reality, of course, it wasn't anything like that, but my sister, like me, was always determined to get her own way.

To begin with, I was very unhappy at school. I didn't see Angela very much at all; she was so much older than me and never wanted to have anything to do with her annoying little sister. We were the only Jewish girls there and I often felt like an outsider. We did everything that the other girls did – going along to morning prayers, that kind of thing, but we never kneeled. I suppose it was our way of keeping our religious identity. Even so, I quite enjoyed going to church and singing in church choirs. I always thought the hymns were beautiful, so it wasn't all bad.

In that first year while we were in Exeter, my parents would often come to visit us at the weekends and would stay at the very smart Rougemont Hotel nearby. I vividly remember laughing at the engraving on the hotel's wine glasses: 'This glass has been stolen from the Rougemont Hotel.' I used to think it was so funny. Who on earth would steal glasses from a hotel? Especially when they had words like that written on them! Irony was obviously lost on me at the time.

For the first few years at school I was bullied. The other girls could be quite cruel and would call me Baby Elly because I was such a chubby little thing. It was terribly upsetting and I often felt homesick. At times like this, I couldn't understand why my parents had decided to abandon me and would feel very sorry for myself. I suppose it didn't help that I wasn't remotely academic. The school had a very high achievement history and good success rates for entry to the top universities. But anything like maths, geography, history or science didn't interest me in the slightest. I was forever daydreaming.

On the plus side, the school also had a wide range of extra-curricular activities and great facilities, including an auditorium, theatre and music hall with several performance areas – just the thing for a little show-off like me!

My favourite subject was singing and I adored my teacher, Miss Rowe. She had fabulous black hair with a thick black fringe and I remember she had a wonderfully infectious personality. She was always so wonderfully positive and when I started singing, although I didn't really give it much thought at the time, Miss Rowe obviously saw something in me and suggested that I audition for the junior choir. I remember being very serious about it and saying to her, 'But, Miss Rowe, whatever will happen if I don't get in?' She was lovely and said, 'Just wait and see!'

I managed to pass the audition and, from that day onwards, the school choir was my favourite thing about school. Miss Rowe continued to encourage me and got me to sing in all of the different choirs available and made sure I auditioned for the various school productions. We did a number of Gilbert and Sullivan operettas, which were huge fun. Performing on stage was always the highlight of the school year for me. After a year of not excelling in anything academic, I relished being given the opportunity to shine on stage. At last, I could show that I was good at something, rather than being just stupid Baby Elly.

I was still very homesick though, and one day I decided that I would run away. I must have been quite a sensible little girl because I didn't just pack up my satchel and run out of the school gates. Instead, I thought it would be a good idea to write to my father beforehand and let him know what I was planning to do so that he wouldn't worry when I disappeared. I informed him that I would let him know where I was as soon as I arrived, but that I couldn't possibly stay at school for a day longer. My mind was made up. Ever the drama queen!

Of course, there was nothing like mobile phones or emails then, but the post must have been quite efficient as I remember getting a letter back from him almost straight away. I ran into one of the toilet cubicles and tore into the letter to read what he said. I was devastated when I saw the words; 'I am sure you know what you are doing, good luck and let me know where you end up.' I burst into tears. All I had wanted him to say was: 'Don't worry, bubele, I'm coming to bring you home!'

After my 'running away' episode, the head teacher, Miss Brake (whose nickname for some reason was Cherub), really looked after me. Perhaps my father had helped me after all and had written to her to say that I was finding it tough. From that day onwards, she was always very kind to me and kept an eye on me. I remember that, whenever there was a thunderstorm, she would come and hunt me out and make sure that I was OK because I was terrified of them.

It's not surprising therefore that, when I was at school, I used to live for the holidays. For years I had a terrible fear of flying and so we would rarely go abroad, even though my parents tried to reassure me that it was very safe. Everything seemed to point otherwise, however, and I remember that one time when I had been persuaded to go to Paris for the weekend, the flight was cancelled and I saw it as an omen that we shouldn't travel by plane at all. It was silly, I know, and nowadays I'm a lot better about flying, but back then it was a different story.

Therefore, in our school holidays, if we weren't going to Woburn Sands, we would often go to Bournemouth with a group of my parents' friends. We would always stay in the same two or three hotels – The Normandie, Green Park and Majestic – and, because we were such regular guests, the hotels became like a home from home. Being Jewish, we never celebrated Christmas in the traditional way, so a whole crowd of us would go to Bournemouth during the Christmas break and we would have a whale of a time. All the children would put on little concerts together, dance and play table tennis. I remember that one year the owner of The Normandie hotel took me for a flight in his helicopter – how glamorous was that! But goodness knows how he managed to persuade me to go with my phobia. I suppose at that time an offer like that would have been too good to resist.

Bournemouth has always been a very special place for me and, in later years, when I was much older, I would go back there for a week here and there – generally when I had split up with a boyfriend. I'd take a little suitcase and a tapestry kit and shut myself away to take my mind off my broken heart. Judging by the amount of cushions I made, I think my heart was broken far too many times!

My mother's cousin lived in Paris, and one year during my school holiday we went there for Christmas. Angela was 18 and so had left school already. One day during our stay, we heard my mother's friend and her son Jerzy would be joining us for dinner. Angela and I were both terribly excited as we had heard that he was very handsome. (Indeed, later in life, Jerzy wrote an autobiography, entitled *Saved By My Face*, in which he recounted how he had been sent to a concentration camp and had been spared the gas chamber because he didn't look Jewish.) My sister and I were both bowled over when we met Jerzy as he was indeed very handsome, and the family encouraged me to sing while he accompanied me on the piano. He was a very accomplished pianist and could have gone on to become a professional musician had he wanted to. I remember having a lovely time, but Angela was extremely taken with him. That night, she set her sights on Jerzy and, six months later, they married.

Meanwhile, I was still at school and, although I was rotten at my studies, I was quite sporty – I loved netball, hockey, tennis and swimming – and of course I lived for singing. To this end, the highlight of my entire school life was when I got the lead role of Coco in the school production of *The Mikado* when I was 16. I loved every second of being in the spotlight on stage. My parents came to see me and it was so wonderful hearing the audience cheering for me. It was their reaction that made me realise that I wanted to sing – and from that moment on I was determined to make a career out of it. I knew that I wouldn't do very well in my school exams, but I was confident about my singing gift.

Luckily, my parents gave me a lot of encouragement about my ambition and never tried to change my mind when I said I wanted to leave school. I was so relieved to get away from boring lessons in which I had no interest. In those days, it wasn't unusual for people to leave school at 16. Some would start work or apprenticeships, others would go to commercial college and learn typing skills or suchlike. There were lots of opportunities and it certainly wasn't like it is now with everyone being encouraged to go on to study A Levels and go to university. There was no stigma then about leaving school with very few academic qualifications.

During the summer after I left school, my parents and I went on holiday to Paris. I vividly remember climbing to the top of the Eiffel Tower and triumphantly throwing my school hat off into the air like a Frisbee. To me, it was the symbol that school life was over and that my real life was about to begin. As you may have gathered, I always rather enjoyed making dramatic gestures!

CHAPTER 6

With school behind me, I got a place on a course at the Guildhall School of Music and Drama, based in the City of London. It was a two-year course that combined acting and singing, but I was to really concentrate on the singing aspect. If I could have done, I would have just sung all day and done nothing else.

The Guildhall was highly respected and I felt very lucky to be there. I learned a great deal, and soon I was being asked to sing at people's weddings. I also got involved with amateur dramatics productions and started to put on little shows with my friends for charity. That thrilled my parents, as charity was such a big thing in their lives, and thrilled me, of course, because I loved performing.

Towards the end of my course at the Guildhall, I fell for a young violinist called Peter. He was my first love and I was head over heels about him. He was very handsome and I was totally swept up in the romance of it all. I could see myself performing on great stages around the world with Peter accompanying me on his beautiful violin. To me, it was the real deal – or so I thought at the time – but as Peter wasn't Jewish there was no way that my parents were ever going to permit the relationship to go any further. I knew there was no point in making a fuss about it. I never disobeyed my family; that just wasn't the done thing in those days. As much as I thought I was in love with Peter, I loved and respected my parents, and that was that. I still lived at home and to all intents and purposes I was still very much their little girl. People didn't grow up and move away from home quite so quickly in those days.

Even though it was likely that I would marry a Jewish boy at some stage or other, my family was never particularly observant. I think that the fact my mother and father had both been brought up in very strict and observant families – and had been persecuted so much growing up in Poland – meant they were more ambivalent about religion with us. Yes, we would always have Friday night supper and we kept all of the holidays, but other parts of our lifestyle were much more relaxed.

After I completed my course at the Guildhall, my parents paid for me to have private lessons from a celebrated singing teacher called Mark Raphael, who had come to England from Poland. He had been director of music at the West London Synagogue during the war and had even broadcast a programme of Mendelssohn's songs on the Home Service in 1941. It was quite a thrill and a great opportunity to be tutored by him.

Mark started to hone my soprano voice into more of an operatic style, and whenever I got the opportunity I would sing in public. He had the most amazing ear and quickly detected my musical strengths and weaknesses. I was always sent home with lots of exercises to practise before my next lesson and I always worked very hard. I had found the thing that I knew I wanted to do for the rest of my life. I had set my heart on becoming a professional opera singer and, for the first time, it was actually a pleasure to do my homework!

Mark encouraged me to record some 78rpm records, so one day the two of us went along to a recording studio in London and I sang four or five pieces of music that were pressed as records. It was very exciting and glamorous, and I felt like a proper singer as I performed the works by Hugo Wolf and Schubert. I also recorded some more modern tracks, including 'I Got You Under My Skin' and 'Oh My Beloved Daddy (O Mio Babbino Caro)'. Funnily enough, many years later, I re-recorded 'I Got You Under My Skin' with my granddaughter Katie. She would have been a similar age to when I originally recorded the record. We 'blocked out' Frank Sinatra's voice and Katie and I sang the vocals with the Nelson Riddle Orchestra playing for us in the background! As you can imagine, the quality of the recording wasn't exactly perfect, as it was the original scratchy version from all those years ago, but it was great fun all the same.

At the time I originally made the recordings, I was around 18. I never expected to release them and have a hit record or anything like that, it was just a kind of training exercise. At this stage, though, I wanted to earn some money and decided to try to get a job. As I had no particular qualifications, I went to work for a company in Park Lane, selling, of all things, carbon paper. It didn't take me long to find out how hard it was being a saleswoman, especially when you are selling something as boring as carbon paper – and so off I went to visit my father, who duly purchased enough carbon paper to last him for the next ten years! With a great sale under my belt, I continued to press on with my job, until one day one of the bosses got a little bit too free with his hands … Screaming hysterically, I ran all the way to my father's office. Needless to say, that was the end of my carbon paper career.

I then worked for my father, who had re-established his fur business in London. He also had a number of rental properties that he had bought together with his friend Sam Green, and I helped out there with the administration work. It suited me fine. It was around this time that I discovered the 'family secret' about how my parents had met.

While I was working for my father's business, I also started helping out with some of his charity work. Throughout his life, my father was a great philanthropist and at that time of my life he was particularly involved with the Jewish Blind Society. I loved helping him with his work and I decided to set up my own part of the charity, which I called the White Stick Aid Committee. My friends and I would often visit the Rokefield home for the blind in Surrey to read to the residents there, and our committee ran functions in order to raise money for them. I don't really know how I learned how to do it; I suppose it all harked back to those days in Bournemouth when my friends and I would put on little shows. Only this time, I charged the audience to watch.

At the time, of course, I didn't realise that charity work was going to play a bigger and bigger part in my life as I got older. It was just great knowing that good was coming out of doing something that we all really enjoyed.

I remember one event that we had put on at a hotel near Maidenhead and we felt that we hadn't raised enough money. I challenged everyone to dive into the swimming pool fully clothed to raise some extra money, but nobody was prepared to do it, apart from … yes, you guessed it, yours truly. I managed to raise nearly £50 just for getting wet and spoiling my best dress, though I got a terrible dressing-down from my parents afterwards. Oh well, all part of the learning process.

Along with helping my father with his businesses and chairing the White Stick Aid Committee, I was still determined to have a proper singing career one day. In 1952, I appeared in a show at the Vaudeville Theatre in London called *Do Me a Favour*, and shortly afterwards I was approached by an impresario who produced some very successful radio shows at the time. He offered me a job on a touring radio show and I was thrilled to bits and very excited.

Sadly, though, it wasn't to be. The job would have meant leaving home and travelling around the country to perform in the shows and, no surprise, my parents were totally against it. I didn't resent them for refusing to let me go; I just hoped that a more suitable opportunity would come up in the future. There was talk of my going to study in Italy, and my mother said she would chaperone me if this was what I chose to do, but eventually I decided against it as I was having such a lovely time at home.

Although my parents encouraged my singing, I think they really hoped I would get married and then just sing occasionally as a hobby. Neither of them was remotely musical, so I suppose they didn't really understand what singing meant to me. They were happiest when I was with all of my friends doing my charity work and not taking life too seriously.

Meanwhile, I had also been roped in to help with a number of other charity committees, including the Silver Spoon Committee for Youth Aliyah and the Marylebone Committee. We used to have dances and other fundraising events, and the Marylebone Committee often put on amateur variety shows, which naturally I was very involved with, singing and dancing. The fact that I was able to raise money while I was doing the thing I loved most in the world was so special to me. The other benefit to all this was that all of a sudden I had a very large wonderful circle of friends.

At that time, I used to go to many charity dinner dances, usually with my best friend Jackie Curtis. We did everything together, and when we were teenagers we even lived in flats opposite each other. One of my most vivid memories is of an evening at the great room of the Grosvenor House Hotel when the band started playing 'The Charleston' – cries went up in the room of 'Where's Morella and Jackie?' as we were famous for our Charleston. It so happens that we were already on the floor showing everyone how it was done – or rather making a spectacle of ourselves …

(I think back over 50 years and the wonderful friendship that Jackie and I enjoyed until our lives were to take different directions. She was a fun, genuine and sincere friend. She was my bridesmaid and good memories of her will always stay in my mind. I look back and smile. Sadly, Jackie died on 16 December 2007, aged 64.)

I really had a charmed life back then and I was so incredibly lucky. I seemed to be either working for my father, organising charity events, or having fun with friends. I was also treated to a lot of fabulous holidays. One time my parents and I went on the maiden cruise of the *Moledet* to Haifa in Israel. I remember it was a super trip and most evenings I would end up entertaining the other 200 passengers singing songs such as 'Blue Moon' and 'Waltz of My Heart'.

On another holiday in the South of France, I remember I had persuaded my father to let me drive his sleek grey Armstrong Siddeley. By this time, my mother had failed her test about 20 times already, so, after much pestering – and the fact that my father wanted to have 40 winks – he allowed me to take the wheel. I remember I was wearing a low-cut neckline and zooming along at about 90mph when a wasp flew straight down my front. The only thing I could think to do was to squash it into my stomach, so that I could concentrate on keeping the car on the road – and avoid killing the three of us. I remember that I expertly managed to avoid a collision but the wasp sting made me look about 20 months' pregnant and was incredibly sore. Not surprisingly, my father didn't stay asleep while all this was going on and after that he was strangely reluctant to let me drive him again for a while! All part of growing up I suppose.

(By the way, my mother passed her test many years later, but after various adventures – including taking the wrong exit off the M1 and ending up in Luton – my father was reluctant to let her drive too.)

In 1949, my parents did something absolutely extraordinarily out of character and allowed me to go on holiday to Knokke in Belgium with Jackie and two other friends. Finally, I thought, they were accepting the fact that I was growing up and that they really should be able to trust that I would not do anything stupid. We had a great time, although we probably ate far too many of their wonderful chocolates and pastries, but that was the extent of our naughty behaviour.

When I was 21, I got engaged to Harry, an Austrian who I met through one of my charity committees. We had many things in common, but I really should never have got engaged to him as he was much older than me. He was crazy about me, though, and I stupidly let the engagement go on for far too long because he really was so lovely to me and I didn't want to upset him. Naively, I had thought it would naturally burn itself out. However, my subtle hints obviously weren't subtle enough. I was hoping that he would give me up rather than the other way round; that way would have been much easier for me, but that didn't happen, so eventually I had to force the issue and got my mother to help out. I know, I'm a coward. My poor mother quickly got used to dealing with my romantic whims.

I was still doing my charity work, going to Rokefield, going to social events and generally thoroughly enjoying myself, even though my parents were pretty strict about what time I had to be home and who I went out with. I always had to be back by 10.30pm and woe betide me if I was ever later than that. I reckon that was the reason there were many Saturdays that I stayed at home. I didn't rebel against it though, and always tried to respect my parents' wishes, but I have to admit it was sometimes hard to tear myself away when I was having fun – especially those nights at the Grosvenor Hotel doing the Charleston!

CHAPTER 7

It was through one of my good friends, Monica Levinson, that I first met Lawrence Fisher. It was 1956 and we were at her 21st birthday party in Hendon, north London. I was in my early twenties at the time and had known Monica for quite a while, having met her through various charity committees that we had worked on together. We were great friends – and still are now, 60 years later – but, truth be told, I hadn't wanted to go to the party that night as I had another date lined up.

It turned out to be a lovely party. There was lots of dancing and socialising, and there was a great crowd of people there. I spent the evening chatting and dancing and generally having a great time, and then, around halfway through, I was introduced to Lawrence. We had never met before and, as I was later to discover, he too hadn't really wanted to be there that night as he also had a date planned. Thank goodness the stars were aligned!

Lawrence was about 5 feet 8 inches so he wasn't exactly what you would call tall, but he was very fit (I later learned he played rugby for Middlesex in his youth). The thing that most struck me about him was that he had beautiful twinkling brown eyes. He was a lovely-looking man. As soon as I met him, I knew he was a really special person, so warm and friendly. I could tell he was totally genuine. He didn't have a bad bone in his body.

'You Make Me Feel So Young' by Frank Sinatra was playing when Lawrence asked me to join him for a dance. He was 13 years older than me, and I suppose I must have appeared very young to him. That didn't bother me at all though, as he was an incredible gentleman – a very gentle man. Plus, he was a lovely dancer. What with Frank Sinatra, the lovely party and his dancing, we immediately clicked and Lawrence and I ended up spending most of the evening together. It wasn't love at first sight or anything earth shattering like that; I just thought he was very nice, we got on very well and it was a super party.

Everyone referred to him as 'Lovely Lawrence' – it was something that would stay with him throughout his life – but, as I say, I wasn't head over heels from the moment I met him. Through my charity committees and my circle of friends, I had lots of male friends at that time, and I didn't think anything more of it really. At the end of the evening, he took my phone number and said that he would give me a call. I didn't think much more about it to be honest – in those days, you would swap numbers all the time and there was never any commitment to follow up with a call. It was just the done thing.

In any case, I was going away with Jackie to Cattolica in Italy the following week, so I was full of plans for the holiday. I didn't even entertain the idea of a new romance. There were so many parties and little flirtations going on.

True to his word though, Lawrence called me the day after the party and we arranged to meet up a couple of times for coffee before I went away. We had a very nice time, but I still wasn't smitten with him. At that stage, I had a few casual boyfriends with whom I would go out on dates, and I never imagined that it would be anything different with Lawrence.

Anyway, off Jackie and I went on holiday and we had a wonderful week. I fell in love with at least two waiters – as did Jackie – and we thoroughly enjoyed ourselves. As I have quite deep olive skin, I've always tanned really easily, so I loved soaking up the sun and living *la dolce vita*. It really was a fabulous girly holiday. Then halfway through the holiday, I got a phone call at the hotel from Lawrence saying he was in Italy! He had decided to fly over because he was missing me and wanted to spend some time with me.

As you can imagine, I wasn't exactly delighted about this; after all, I was having far too much fun with Jackie and all of those handsome Italian waiters. But what could I say? He was there and, yes, it did make me feel special that he had come all the way to Italy to see me. I was flattered – and a little flabbergasted at the same time. It wasn't as if you could just get a last-minute budget airline flight in those days. This was serious stuff.

Of course, the holiday totally changed when he arrived. We were in separate rooms – in those days, you certainly wouldn't share a room with a boyfriend. It was much more formal, you wouldn't have the kind of relationship where you would sleep with anyone before being married (in any case, my mother would have killed me if I had!). Plus I was with Jackie; I couldn't go off with Lawrence and abandon her.

Nevertheless, Lawrence and I had a lovely time getting to know each other as we wandered around the historical sights and ate lots of beautiful Italian food. Jackie was with us, so we made a very happy trio. Gradually, as I spent more time with Lawrence and got to know him better, I realised that he was indeed the sort of person that I should be going out with. He had been brought up in a fairly strict home and his parents were quite old-fashioned, and so it was a very respectful relationship. He always behaved like the perfect gentleman with both of us. Jackie definitely approved!

When the holiday was over, we all came back to London, and Lawrence and I continued to see each other. He worked with his brother Clifford at their father's motorcycle and electrical accessories company, and I carried on working for my charity committees as a volunteer and also for my father's business. It was quite a slow-burner of a relationship, not one of those where you know right from the very start that he's Mr Right and that you are going to end up married. I had already had at least two infatuations that had completely taken my breath away after all, but this felt different.

For their part, my parents were very relieved when I started going on dates with Lawrence as I was a lot easier to live with – I wasn't shouting my love from the rooftops and wailing 'you don't understand' as I had with Peter and Harry. They saw Lawrence as a good, upstanding, trustworthy fellow. As far as they were concerned, he was perfect marriage material, although at the time they did their utmost not to say anything as they didn't want to jinx it. Once we were married, of course, they never tired of telling me what a wonderful choice I had made – how they had known he was the one for me all along, etc. etc.!

Lawrence started joining me on my Sunday outings to Rokefield to visit the home for the blind and it was on one of these trips, around three months after we had first met at Monica's 21st, that he asked me if I would agree to 'be his girl'. I was later to discover that this was his way of asking me to be his 'serious' girlfriend, with a view to one day hopefully becoming engaged and becoming his wife. I don't know if I realised the importance of what he was saying to me at the time – that, in a way, it was effectively a proposal – but I told him I would, on the condition that he promised to carry on coming with me to Rokefield. He immediately agreed. He knew I was passionate about my work there and his agreeing to help me with it was the key to my heart. I know now that it was a ridiculous way to answer him, but it was the one that I gave and it felt right at the time.

Lovely Lawrence was over the moon. It was extremely flattering to feel so special and after that we became a proper couple. I just knew that he was right for me. I also knew that my parents would be really happy – for once – about whom I had chosen. He was everything that they wanted the man I married to be – gentle, kind and very respectable.

Being the kind of parents that they were, my mother and father made it plain to me that they thought it was high time that I got married or I risked being left on the shelf. People got married younger in those days and, being in my mid-twenties, I was practically an old maid in their eyes. Added to this, Lawrence got on so well with my parents that everyone was thrilled we were together.

And to think it was all thanks to Monica and that 21st birthday party that I nearly missed.

My friends were all part of the same crowd that went to Rokefield to help out on Sunday afternoons, and Lawrence fitted in beautifully with everyone. I didn't know anyone that didn't like him and he had a wide circle of very loyal friends – many from his school years. For a man of his age, he was still quite shy and had only ever had one serious girlfriend before me.

Lawrence learned to fly aircraft in 1944 (I still have his beautifully written log book from that time) and he flew Spitfires and several other aircraft while serving with the RAF, but he certainly wasn't the typical cocky Brylcreem boy. At that time, there was a real RAF type, all bravado and banter, but my gentle, beautiful Lawrence wasn't like that at all.

CHAPTER 8

A few months after he had asked me to be his girl, Lawrence and I decided to get married. We didn't have a long engagement. In those days (before sex before marriage!) people tended to get married more quickly and, besides, we knew that it was right for us. We named the day as Tuesday, 15 December 1957. For Jewish people, Tuesdays are thought to be a lucky day, so that was the day of the week we picked and we quickly began making plans. I was so excited. I had fallen very much in love with Lawrence and I loved the idea of being married to him.

As was tradition, the invitations were sent out six weeks before the wedding. My parents were away a lot of the time. My father was suffering with chronic asthma by then and would spend as much time as he could abroad, out of the cold, during the autumn and winter months. I was holding the fort at my father's showroom while they were away and working in the West End meant I could pop out to buy various bits and pieces for the wedding and my honeymoon. It was such an exciting time for me.

One day I was at work when I got a phone call from a man called Frank Martin. He said that he had been recommended to get in touch with my father's company through some mutual South African friends. He said his wife had recently had an operation and was coming out of hospital at the weekend. This was a Thursday and he wanted to surprise her with a mink coat. When I told him that my father was away, he said, 'Not to worry, I have other people that I can call about it.' But being the born saleswoman – or, at least, so I thought – I said I wouldn't hear of it and invited him up to the showroom, saying I would be only too pleased to help him find the perfect gift for his wife.

The following morning, Frank came up to the showroom and he was utterly charming; tall, dark and very handsome. We had coffee and discussed all the people that we knew in common. He seemed lovely and totally genuine. I was so bowled over that I didn't notice that he was just agreeing with everything I said rather than actually offering any real information.

He spotted the wedding invitations on my father's desk and, since we were getting on so well, I decided to ask him and his wife to the wedding as well. I told him that it was going to be quite a big party and, as he would know so many of the people who were going to be there, it would be lovely to have him there, too.

Meanwhile, I modelled some of the furs for him. He couldn't make up his mind between two of our top-price coats. They were both full-length minks, and were sumptuous and beautiful. In those days, it was usual for jewellers and furriers to provide customers with goods on approval, and he asked me and my father's manager, Dick, if it would be all right for him to take a coat for his wife to see if she liked it. I remember thinking, 'There's no way that she won't absolutely love it. It's the finest quality full-length mink coat, for goodness' sake. What could she possibly not like about it!' But I kept quiet. I was so excited that I had practically made a sale.

Frank assured us that he would return the coat after the weekend so that it could be finished and made ready for his wife. In those days, the customer would choose which type of lining they would like to have in a coat or jacket, often having it monogrammed with the lady's name or initials at the same time. To that end, they weren't 'finished' coats. This is an important fact, as I was later to discover.

As Frank couldn't decide which one of two coats he most liked, Dick and I discussed the idea of his taking both to show his wife. In today's money, that would have been at least £4000 worth of goods that we were essentially handing over for nothing. But Frank was a canny customer. To ensure that we didn't think he was stealing from us, he gave us the name and phone number of the hotel where he was staying and he encouraged me to call there to check he was who he said he was – which, of course, I did. Dick and I had no doubt that Frank was being completely honest with us – after all, he and my father had so many mutual friends!

When he left, Dick and I were both quite pleased with ourselves. I remember doing a little dance of joy around the showroom, and we looked forward to telling my father on his return that we had secured a great sale. Dick was one of those people that was so honest that, if he noticed a halfpenny difference in the petty cash, he would stay all night to work out the discrepancy. To this end, I felt quite secure about what we had done. If he had any doubts that Frank wasn't 100 per cent trustworthy, we would never have done what we did.

When I spoke to my mother later that day, she was horrified that we had given away not one but two mink coats. She had absolutely no concept of business and the idea of letting people have goods on approval, and I tried to put her mind at rest and reassured her that it was the kind of thing that was done all the time, and that my father would be really pleased at how we had handled the situation.

Thankfully, when I did catch up with him and he heard our story, he was perfectly happy about the deal.

On the following Monday morning, the phone rang and it was Frank Martin. Dad was back at work by now and he and Frank seemed to get on like a house on fire as Frank explained that he was held up at the hospital that day. He asked if it would be OK to come on the Tuesday instead to finalise the deal. He told my father that he was so delighted with his London shopping that he wanted to show his gratitude to us and invited my father and me to have lunch with him at Claridge's Hotel. He said he would meet us at my father's showroom at 1pm on the following day and that we would go on from there.

Well, one o'clock Tuesday came and went and by the time it was 2pm my father suggested that we went downstairs to the local café for a sandwich. By then, it was beginning to dawn on us that we may have been conned. My father sent his driver to the hotel address that we had been given by Frank and when he got there he was one of many hoping to find the elusive Frank Martin. Apparently, he had already checked out – along with a collection of fine clothes and jewellery that he had managed to scam from other well-known stores.

We later discovered that, when Frank had initially called the showroom on that fateful Friday, he had literally just pulled off another theft at a jeweller's who had allowed him a similar 'goods on approval' arrangement. Meanwhile, I was absolutely mortified – not only for stupidly being taken in by him, but also for giving him a wedding invitation, which had my parents' home address for the RSVP. I was extremely upset that I hadn't had the sense to see through it, but, as a professional con man, he knew all the tricks of his dodgy trade.

My father contacted his solicitor to find out if we were covered for insurance purposes. Terrible news: his solicitor said that, as we had essentially given Frank the coats, my father's company would not be able to claim the money back for them. Devastated, my father then contacted other solicitors, but they all said the same thing. You can understand why really.

However, my tenacious father eventually contacted a very well-known firm of solicitors who found a loophole in the law. Because the stolen coats were unlined – and therefore unfinished – my father would be able to claim on insurance. Phew! His claim was finally settled and at the end of the day all was well.

Meanwhile, Dick and I had many visits to Scotland Yard to look at pictures of known conmen and there was one that we felt looked similar. They didn't catch him straight away, but, lo and behold, several years later, Frank Martin was caught and convicted. He was no longer tall, dark and handsome by then!

CHAPTER 9

After the nightmare of the previous six weeks and all the burglary shenanigans, our actual wedding day went off without a hitch. It was an incredibly lavish affair. We got married early afternoon in Brondesbury Synagogue in north London and thankfully the weather stayed fine. Although it was a very crisp December day, we were glad it was virtually all held indoors. After the service in the synagogue, we had a huge reception for 200 guests at the famous Savoy Hotel in the centre of the West End. Everything was perfect. I had a magnificent silk taffeta dress with lace and hand-stitched beading, which was designed by Neymar, a very big name at the time.

My friend Jackie and Angela's daughters Karen and Ginette were bridesmaids, and we had two page boys, Stephen and Graham, who were Lawrence's nephews. Lawrence's brother Clifford was his best man and he had six ushers: Angela's husband Jerzy, Lawrence's brother-in-law Oswald and his longtime friends Bernard Friend, Charles Berman, Jimmy Tournoff and Ronnie Hanbury.

We had a band playing fabulous music – there were lots of Frank Sinatra and Glenn Miller numbers – a lavish champagne reception, a massive sit-down dinner, stunning flowers and fantastic speeches. And of course we danced to 'You Make Me Feel So Young', the song that had brought us together.

I still have the book with the list of guests at my wedding and it is wonderful to look at and reminisce. The toast to my parents was given by my father's friend Norman Hirshfield – he and his lovely wife Iris were on the Rokefield Aid Committee with my parents. Many years later, we were to become connected again when my daughter got married.

Although our wedding was quite grand and had so many guests, it still felt very special as we involved lots of close friends and family in the ceremony. I will never forget the speech my father gave. He was so nervous and emotional that he had the piece of paper in his hand one moment and it was on the floor the next. He had dropped it as he was shaking so much. Then he had to try to remember what he was going to say while everyone egged him on, the poor thing. However, he handled it very well.

Lawrence's speech was very romantic and very beautiful. In fact, the whole day was absolutely perfect. Everyone danced until midnight. It was every girl's dream wedding. My dear mother was so happy that her baby had finally got herself married and had chosen such a nice man that she had tears in her eyes all day. Her happiness really shone through.

Unfortunately, my friend Monica, who had introduced me to Lawrence in the first place, was unable to come to my wedding due to illness. So I was very honoured many years later when she and her husband Dennis asked me to be godmother to their youngest daughter, Josephine.

Lawrence and I had planned to go abroad for our honeymoon, but I was still terribly nervous about flying. It was silly, I know, and nowadays I'm a lot better about flying, but back then it was a different story. Instead, we went to my beloved Bournemouth for two weeks, which was super. After the honeymoon, we planned to go straight to the wedding of other dear friends, Pamela and Lionel. I had known Lionel all my life as our parents were close friends and Lionel's Mother Sunshine, as she was known, secretly hoped that he and I would hit it off when we grew up. But, although we were always good friends, as soon as Lionel met Pamela, she was the only girl he ever wanted.

While Lawrence and I were on honeymoon, my parents came to see us, claiming that they had been on their way to Eastbourne and just decided to pay us a visit. I never expected my parents to be part of my honeymoon, but there you go. You didn't argue with my parents!

To make things even more awkward, my mother, who was never backwards in coming forward, asked all sorts of personal questions, and then Angela turned up for a quick visit too and we all ended up going to the cinema together. It certainly wasn't a conventional honeymoon, and I couldn't help thinking that maybe we should have gone abroad after all. But through it all, Lawrence, in his usual wonderful way, didn't mind. Anything that made me happy made him happy, too.

CHAPTER 10

On returning home from our honeymoon in Bournemouth, Lawrence and I were very excited about moving into our first home together. It was a new apartment in a very pretty area of London, Maida Vale, and it meant we would be near to my parents. Unfortunately, we got back to London to discover that the sale had fallen through while we were away. We decided that the best idea was to rent a furnished flat while we looked for somewhere else and, luckily, we found a lovely place nearby in St John's Wood, where we lived for about six months.

We settled into married life, with me playing house and Lawrence going off to work every day. It was around then that we started having bridge lessons and could be up until 3am playing because we got so hooked. Over 50 years later, I am still learning!

Lawrence and I would have happily lived in the flat in St John's Wood for longer than six months, but I discovered I was pregnant so we had to quickly find a family house. The pregnancy came as quite a surprise as we had not intended to start a family quite so soon. Luckily, we found the perfect home for us in Hendon in north London, and were able to move in straight away. Everything seemed to fall into place so easily.

The pregnancy itself was fine, except I started putting on rather too much weight. After just two months, everyone knew I was expecting as I was really quite a size. It really didn't help that my mother would always ply me with delicious treats whenever I visited. By the time I had gone full term, I had put on five-and-a-half stone, which would never be allowed today; it was quite a weight to lug around. My gynaecologist was a very eminent doctor called George Pinker (he would later become the Queen's specialist), but he never seemed overly concerned. I guess at that time there wasn't such an emphasis on eating correctly throughout pregnancy. Everyone just said, 'You're eating for two' and piled up my plate with more and more calories. I didn't mind in the slightest at the time, but it was hard to shift later.

Added to this, the birth was very late. Although I had been due at the end of December 1958, in fact, the baby didn't arrive until over a month later. In late January, I was told that the birth would have to be induced, and yet still nothing happened. Finally, at 12 noon on Sunday, 1 February 1959, I had a Caesarean and my beautiful daughter Amanda was born, although right from the start we decided to call her Mandy. To me, she was the most perfect thing I had ever held in my arms and I fell in love with her from the moment I saw her. Lawrence did, too. The pair of us were smitten.

I would have preferred to have had a natural birth rather than a Caesarean. My mother had always told me that there was nothing more miraculous, but my darling little girl just didn't seem to want to be born that way. As soon as I held her in my arms and saw her perfect little face, it put everything into perspective. She was certainly worth the wait.

Lawrence and I were both so excited about our new baby

daughter. A week after she was born, driving home from the maternity hospital in Paddington, we kept showing our new baby to other drivers. Lawrence kept winding down the window and shouting, 'That's my baby, that's my baby!' Needless to say, other drivers probably thought we were slightly strange, to say the least, but we didn't care – we just wanted to show her off! We felt so lucky to have this beautiful little bundle. In those days, before safety belts – I sat in the front seat with my Mandy in my arms. Health and safety would have a few things to say about that now.

Unfortunately, our euphoria didn't last. A few days later, I started feeling very unwell. I was unable to breastfeed Mandy and I felt very woozy. Because I had been given so many stitches after the Caesarean, I was unable to pick her up as it would be too much strain on my tummy and I was very upset about the whole thing. I wanted to bond with her as much as possible, but I just felt too weak. Imagine not being able to hold your own baby? I felt like such a failure. To make things worse, my stiff upper-lipped mother just told me to pull myself together.

As things got worse, we called Mr Pinker. He came to see us and it turned out that I had infected stitches and had to have an immediate procedure at home, there and then, followed by a course of very strong antibiotics to wipe out the infection before it flooded my body. When my mother discovered how severe the infection was, she felt terribly guilty for having said I should just pull myself together. We all knew she wasn't always the most considerate person when it came to illness, as I had previously discovered with the burn incident when I was very young.

With the right medication, my stitches healed, time passed and the three of us got into a very happy routine. Even if I had initially missed out on cuddles when Mandy was very tiny, we soon made up for it. Bonding was easy and we enjoyed a lovely family life together. Lawrence was a very hands-on father and had no qualms

Above: A chubby me in 1935.

Below left: My parents in June, 1943.

Below right: Lawrence looking very handsome in his RAF uniform, 1946.

The day of my engagement to Lawrence, 1957.

Lawrence and me on our
wedding day, 15 December 1957.

Above left: With Lawrence and Jackie in Cattolica, 1959.

Above right: Mandy, my favourite model, aged four in 1963.

Below: Lawrence boating on the River Thames, 1969.

Above: Alzheimer's former president Jonathan Miller speaking at a charity film show in 1981.

Below: With Princess Alexandra and John Lubbock, conductor of the St John's Smith Square orchestra, at an Alzheimer's event at St James' Palace in 1993.

Above: Me and my great friend Sonia in 2007.

Below: March 2007 House of Lords luncheon with celebrity guests including Britt Ekland, Richard Briers, Lynda Bellingham, Kevin Whately and Sally Lindsay.

Above left: Gerald and me on our wedding day 29 July 1986.

Above right: With Gerald at the Society of Jewish Lady Golf Captains, Selsdon Park in 1985.

Below: On holiday in Spain with Mandy and grandchildren Katie and Ollie in 2000.

With Mandy
in 2008.

about changing nappies and being fully involved. And I always had extra help from my parents. My father had retired by then and they were now living in Hove in Sussex, but they also had a pied-à-terre in town, so we saw plenty of them. I felt incredibly loved and supported and it was a very happy time for all of us.

Because I had put on so much weight during my pregnancy and was still over five stone heavier than before, I went to see a diet doctor in Harley Street. I remember it was very expensive but it certainly had the desired effect on my weight, which came off very quickly indeed. At that time, not much was known about diet pills – all I knew was that I was quite hyper while I was on them, and the house had never looked so clean! I didn't feel particularly good about myself the whole time I was taking the pills, though, and, after I had dropped the weight, I very quickly came off them. I worried that in the long term they could be very bad for me as it's just not normal to be able to lose so much so quickly. I did put some weight back on once I was off the pills, but it stabilised after a while. I wish I could say it was the last time I was ever on a diet, but there were many, many more to follow!

In the main, life was good – very good, in fact – and I had fully intended to have more children. I had always dreamed of having a large family, like all the Goodkinds from my childhood. Lots of noise, fun and games, that's what I had always dreamed of. But two years later, things started to go seriously wrong …

CHAPTER 11

In 1961, I noticed I had a little rash on my hands so I went to see my GP about it. I wouldn't normally have bothered him with something so trivial, but I am very glad that I did as, while I was with him, I also mentioned I had a small lump on my neck. He examined me and was so concerned that he immediately arranged for me to see a specialist the following day. I just took it in my stride, thinking that everything would be OK. I never once thought it would be anything to be seriously worried about. After all, the lump wasn't at all painful.

The following day, I went into hospital where the growth was investigated and, unbeknown to me, discovered to be malignant, so I was referred immediately for emergency surgery. My mother and father were in a terrible state about it, but I duly went along to have the operation, thinking that would be that. Unfortunately, during the procedure, a secondary growth was discovered on my thyroid gland and so another surgery was scheduled to remove it. Even then, I didn't start getting unduly concerned about it; I was being treated for whatever it was, and I wasn't in any pain.

Nobody at that stage told me that I had cancer. In those days, the very word spelled the end because there was so little chance of surviving it. So, throughout the whole process, the actual word 'cancer' was never even mentioned. As far as I was concerned, it was just a growth that had to be dealt with. Even though I was 27, I was still very much under my parents' wing, and they took the decision that the C word was never to be uttered in front of me. Although Lawrence and I never had any secrets between us, in this instance, he didn't share what he knew.

The surgery to remove the growth was quite straightforward. I just went into hospital, had a quick op and came out again – nothing dramatic. What was more stressful was the fact that I had to follow up the procedure with cobalt radiotherapy treatment. I routinely undertook the treatment four times a week for six weeks at a clinic in London. It's crazy, but, even though it went on for so long, I can't really remember any details about it – it's almost as if I was determined to forget it as soon as it happened.

What I do know is the treatment wasn't anywhere near as severe or sickening as modern chemotherapy, so I didn't lose my hair or suffer any really hideous side effects. That's not to say I didn't feel dreadful throughout the treatment. I tried to stay positive, while my parents and Lawrence anxiously looked after me and took care of Mandy. And all the while, even though I had to have treatment several times a week, I was kept totally in the dark about how severe the problem really was. Nobody talked about the long-term prognosis or the fact it could be life-threatening, and I suppose by not asking outright I kept myself in denial, too. It was probably only a couple of years later that I discovered I had actually had cancer.

The whole thing is a blur. Like so many devastating times of my life, I have a seemingly built-in capacity to blank them out. In retrospect, I suppose I just followed the routine of treatments in the same way that I had with the deep x-ray sessions to remove the scarring on my neck. It was just something I had to do, so I got on with it.

I don't know if I was stupid, but I don't remember ever being overwhelmed about what I was going through. My mother, however, was suffering terribly emotionally. She quickly learned that it was all of those deep x-ray treatments that had triggered the cancer in the first place. She blamed herself for starting the horrible chain of events with the hot poultice. She never forgave herself for causing me so much pain and suffering. In fact, I think she suffered more throughout this period than I did. While I was busy trying to keep positive and matter-of-fact about the whole situation so that I could get on with motherhood as best as I could, she was devastated by what she had inadvertently done to me.

For me, although I hadn't been torn apart emotionally by the notion of cancer, it was the aftermath of the illness that broke my heart. Because of the aggressive treatment, my voice was wrecked and it meant I would never be able to sing again. While I never really thought about the long-term prognosis of my health and whether the cancer would return, I knew that the operation had effectively ended any dreams I had had about rebuilding my singing career. Although my career may have been on the backburner while I was at home being a mum to Mandy, I had hoped that I would eventually return to opera singing one day. So, for me, the consequences far outweighed any suffering caused during the treatment process. Yes, I know it was an incredible blessing that I was able to survive cancer, but when you have held a dream in your heart for the whole of your life – as I had with singing – it feels like a piece of you dies inside.

It was several years before I could even bear to listen to music again and even longer to actually enjoy it. It made me too emotional to think I could never be part of the music world. I sympathise with anyone who has their gift taken from them, and I get angry and frustrated knowing that some people give up their talents for no apparent reason.

Added to being heartbroken that I would never fulfil my dreams of being an opera singer, I was also devastated to discover that I wouldn't be able to have any more children. Even though I had no problems falling pregnant with Mandy, it transpired that the complications I encountered with her birth were a result of problems with my Fallopian tubes. As I had gone on to carry one child, I had hoped that I would go on to conceive again. Lawrence and I did try, but I think I knew in my heart of hearts that I wasn't going to be lucky the second time around. Later, obviously, I discussed it with the doctor and, following more exploratory surgery, it was confirmed that I wouldn't be able to have any more children. Lawrence and I were upset, but we tried to be sanguine about the situation. After all, we had our wonderful daughter Mandy, who was becoming more of a delight every day and the most charming personality we could imagine. How could we dwell on what could have been when we were already so blessed?

CHAPTER 12

As had always been instilled in me, I knew I had to count my blessings and make the most of the cards that had been dealt to me, but, as I faced a different kind of future from the one I had always intended, I started to really struggle emotionally. I battled on while Mandy was a baby, trying to do everything I could for my darling daughter and my lovely husband, but to be honest I was on the brink of becoming seriously depressed.

When Mandy got to three years old – so not as dependent as she had been as a baby – it opened up more of a void in my life that potentially could have been devastating. I had desperately wanted more children and secretly I felt a bit of a failure as a mother. Because I no longer had any potential to sing either, everything was becoming very bleak. Luckily, my dear father was able to help me move on.

At that time, he was still financially fairly comfortable, so he offered to help me set up a business that would help take my mind off my problems. We talked about various options and after much discussion we hit upon the idea of a children's clothes shop. Even though Mandy was still a tot, I had found it hard to find the kind of clothes that I wanted to dress her in, so it seemed to be the answer.

The idea was that rather than a particularly serious business I should treat it more like a hobby. I started looking for suitable premises and found a shop in Temple Fortune in north-west London that I thought would be perfect. It was quite an affluent neighbourhood and there were many families in the area, so I thought it was an ideal location. There was a chemist, a haberdashery and a ladieswear shop, so childrenswear was a perfect fit.

Mind you, the various people I discussed it with thought that nearby Golders Green would be a better option as it was such a busy town centre, but I stuck to my guns and I'm really glad that I did. I was also very lucky as there were two flats above the shop and the rent that I got from them paid for the shop anyway, so it was financially a much better idea for me to be there.

I took great pleasure in sourcing beautiful stock for the shop. I decided to call it Amanda, after my little girl, and filled it with fabulous bridesmaids' dresses, party clothes, page-boy outfits, coats, underwear, tights, socks – you name it, I sold it! It was hard to believe the amount of stock I needed to efficiently run a shop selling children's clothes, but, as it sold clothes for girls from birth to their teens and clothes for boys up to the age of six, that was a lot of growing stages to cover.

My father was such a shrewd businessman and taught me a lot, but, as it was a totally different venture to anything the family had been in before, I had to make up a lot of the business as I went along. I bought to my own taste and hoped that it was what other people would want, too.

Of course, I made plenty of mistakes along the way and there were some amusing incidents. For example, when babygrows first came out, I thought they were such a good idea that I bought every size in one colour – so from one month old until 18 months old, five babygrows in total. Needless to say, when they sold out in a matter of hours, I realised that I had to make bigger orders in future. I immediately put in an order for five of each size in three different colours – 75 in total – and even that was nowhere near enough as people couldn't get enough of them. I think it was one of my best sellers as they just walked off the shelves. I quickly learned the lesson of how important it is to have plenty of stock.

A new shopping centre was being built called Brent Cross and for a while I contemplated opening a shop there. But once the shopping centre was opened, and I had sussed out that the shops there catered for the cheaper end of the childrenswear market, I decided to concentrate on the medium to high end with a much more exclusive stock. At that time there was a label called Rob Roy and they made beautiful coats, which retailed for around £7.50 (which would be more like £175 in today's money). But because it was a very affluent area, they sold well and very shortly I was getting customers from all over the country, including some very wealthy Arabs who loved my merchandise.

I opened the shop on a Tuesday – a lucky day – and I remember that my first sale was a pair of socks at five shillings (I suppose about £5 in today's money). I was absolutely thrilled to bits and telephoned everyone to say that I had made a sale. The cost of the phone calls was probably more than the cost of the socks, but I didn't care! I was on a roll.

Because I wanted to concentrate on high-quality merchandise, I started to visit trade shows all over Europe, including France, Spain, Italy and Germany. It was exactly what I needed to get me back on my feet again and to take my mind off the fact I couldn't have any more children. I had a fabulous time travelling around Europe and building up the business.

The shop went from strength to strength and eventually turned into an incredible success that was to continue for 30 years. By the time I finally retired from the business, I had dressed three generations of families and Amanda had become quite famous locally. Even 25 years after retiring, I still meet and see old customers who remember my gorgeous little shop.

I taught myself book-keeping and I had my own methods for stock control. As I say, I made it up as I went along at the start. But then, as things became more successful, I could start hiring staff. I had a lovely team – some of whom worked with me for many, many years. One lady, Hilda, was with me from day one until the end and we have continued to be great friends right into her nineties. The son of another staff member became my accountant and eventually transferred my handwritten bookkeeping onto the computer. I remember thinking at the time that it was all very 21st century!

I learned customer service as I went along, too. Obviously, there were always awkward customers, but I very quickly created the mantra: 'If you are going to give into them eventually, do it at the start.' It made for a much less stressful life.

My father was a great support and encouraged me every step of the way. He was always such a strong influence on my life – in business and at home. I remember when he came round to the house one Saturday afternoon when I was ironing and watching the horseracing on TV. I had had a little flutter – as I often did at the weekend – but when I told him he wasn't impressed! At all. I quickly learned that the only way to make money was to earn it. Luckily, he didn't remind me about the day I gave away two mink coats to a total stranger!

At Amanda, I prided myself in working hard and selling a whole party outfit from top to toe. For this reason, once I got into the swing of things, I always had masses of stock. But as a result the quiet days made me rather anxious. I worried that things might not pick up and I would have boxes and boxes of childrenswear to find homes for. But the shop achieved its purpose in helping me find a new direction and it gave me a whole new lease of life. I threw myself into it body and soul. It was quite a glamorous position to be in and I loved meeting the customers and seeing the children who came into the shop grow up from toddlers to teens.

I felt part of their lives and the community itself as customers would come into the shop excitedly to find a new party dress or something for a special occasion or a Bar Mitzvah because I sold such unique clothes. I had a regular clientele who came to us from all over. It was always a bit of a treat to come to Amanda and I remember the thrilled looks of little girls when they had a lovely new outfit to take home with them. And, of course, my own daughter Mandy always had lots of lovely dresses – after all, the shop was named after her! We had several fashion shows with Mandy as my star model. She used to love 'helping' in the shop and seemed to have the natural sales gift. Even as a tiny tot, she would encourage people to part with their money, saying, 'I think you should buy this one, it's lovely!'

When she got older, she eventually became my partner in the shop and would be the front person while I took care of the business side. We worked really well together and people used to say we were a good double act because we have exactly the same sense of humour.

At exhibition times, which happened twice a year, I would often be invited out for lunch or dinner by my suppliers. One year I remember thinking that I had never been invited out by Harold Bohrer, one of my suppliers who was also a family friend. I decided to confront him – only jokingly, of course – and told him he was probably the only supplier that had not taken me out for dinner, so he said he would rectify that situation. He invited me to meet him for a drink at the Dorchester Hotel after the exhibition we were attending and said he would book a table for the two of us for dinner at The White Tower.

Armed with this information, I phoned Harold's wife Sybil, and suggested that we had a laugh and played a trick on him. The plan was that she would be at the restaurant with Lawrence before we arrived – as if they were having a secret liaison! She thought it was a great idea and was very happy to go along with this bit of mischief. So, when I met Harold at the Dorchester and he told me that he couldn't get a table there and that we were going to the Empress, I panicked. I tried to phone Sybil to warn her, but couldn't get hold of her – of course, there were no mobile phones in those days. Anyway, I must have been acting strangely because Harold kept asking what on earth was wrong with me.

We left the Dorchester and drove to the Empress. I couldn't believe it when we got there and at our table were Sybil and Lawrence! Sybil had worked the double-double cross and so we managed to pull off the trick. I'll never forget Harold's face as he tried to work out what was going on. Meanwhile, the three of us all tried to keep a straight face until the penny dropped. Such a fabulous memory. I've always loved playing tricks on people!

While I worked hard building up the business with Amanda, Lawrence continued to work for his father's wholesale business, but his father never actually gave him a proper salary, just pocket money. You could say he was pretty old-fashioned, and you would be right! We had never wanted for anything initially – my parents bought our house for us and his parents furnished it, but, as life went on, it became difficult to find enough money for all the household expenses and so on. It was frustrating that Lawrence was just paid pin money when he worked so hard all the time.

Lawrence never complained about this, though; in fact, I can't remember him ever complaining about anything. His brother was a born salesman and had a very bold personality, whereas Lawrence was happy being the calm, diligent one who accepted his lot and just quietly got on with life. He would never rock the boat and went out of his way to avoid any kind of confrontation. In fact, if there was ever any kind of row brewing, he would go for a walk to get away from the tension.

I was frustrated sometimes that he never pushed himself further, but he didn't have that type of character. For this reason, nothing ever seemed to faze or upset him. He was just a good hard-working son, incredibly loyal to his family and a very loving husband and father.

So, although Lawrence wasn't making a lot of money, luckily my children's clothes shop was proving a great success and I was quickly able to open another two branches. It turned out to be the best thing I ever could have done. I had initially thought of Amanda as a bit of a hobby, but later on, when fate took its course, it was to become a necessity, providing the family's lifeline.

CHAPTER 13

When Mandy was about six, we started going on boating holidays with our next-door neighbours, Stanley and Vera Coleman, and their three children. We would hire a couple of boats on the Thames and cruise up the river, mooring up and stopping off at places for lunch, going for walks and generally just laughing and relaxing. We all absolutely loved it, because we didn't care what we looked like and never made any plans for the day, just pootling along the river. The kids would always be thrilled if they saw animals they could pet along the way, and Lawrence would always cook up the most fabulous breakfasts for us. It was such a lovely, special time. We went abroad occasionally too, but it was the boating holidays that we loved best as we all got on so well.

No matter how many years we went on boating holidays, though, we never got to grips with the finer points of boat-handling and we would be forever bumping into other people and getting stuck in locks! We always had adventures and Mandy would have some great 'What I did on my holiday' stories to take back for the new term.

Holidays had always been such special times for me, and I wanted Mandy to have lovely holiday memories too. She used to love visiting her grandparents in Hove – or Nanna and Poppa as she used to call them. She couldn't get enough of my mother's cooking and she absolutely adored my father, who used to call her Mindy. Because I was often very busy in the shop, Mandy would stay with them quite a lot during the school holidays and she loved it as they had a beach hut that she could pretend was her own little house. And, of course, there were things like Punch and Judy shows and donkey rides to entertain her. She was always spoiled because she was the apple of my daddy's eye.

They were very generous grandparents with all their grandchildren, but I am afraid I was a bit strict with them about it and stipulated that Mandy 'must always look at the face before the hands'. In other words, I didn't want her to just assume that people would always buy her gifts in life. But I think that may have backfired a little as one year she rather lost out on presents altogether. I think they took me rather too much at my word and, instead of lavishing her with gifts, they gave her some figs. Sorry, Mandy.

Of course, Mandy was the apple of our eye too, and when she was little very often after Sunday lunch we would all cuddle up in bed and watch the afternoon film together. I think Lawrence was at his happiest when we did this.

Growing up, she went to two Jewish schools, although Lawrence and I weren't particularly religious. As a result, Mandy was the only one of the three of us who had any kind of command of Hebrew. Therefore, she would be the one leading the prayers and taking the service at festival time – a fact my father was always incredibly proud of!

At school, Mandy was quite a tomboy and, like me, wasn't at all academic. But she was always very sporty – give her a ball and she would be happy for the rest of the day. This was to stand her in good stead as she reached her teens.

The love of sports ran in the family and, in 1963, my sister Angela had joined a very smart golf club in Hertfordshire called Dyrham Park Golf and Country Club. She was always talking about how wonderful it was, so, in 1967, we decided to join, too, as it was something we could all do as a family.

We started to have golf lessons, and to begin with I didn't even know which way round the club was meant to go, let alone how to swing it. Luckily, we had a fantastic teacher called Pat Keene. He was so encouraging that eventually I learned not only how to swing the club, but also how to make a shot. I had heard that once you hit a ball you're hooked, and it's absolutely true. I couldn't wait to get out on the actual course, but you had to pass a proficiency test first to prove you knew the golf club rules and etiquette. I probably had about 20 half-hour lessons. I can't remember exactly how long it took to learn, but we were all very determined and I was playing properly within three months.

We all took to it really quickly, and about a year later Lawrence and I played in the very first Dyrham Open – a competition to publicise the club. Amazingly, I won the singles championships and Lawrence and I won the pairs. I remember the trophies were incredible and were presented to us at the Savoy at the very grand annual club dinner and prize-giving ball.

The golf club soon became a very important part of our lives and, at my best, I had a handicap of 16. Local shops in Temple Fortune, where Amanda was located, used to close their shops at lunchtime on a Thursday, so I used to go to the club then, and then again most Sundays. Lawrence played both days at the weekend and Mandy played during the school holidays as much as she could. In fact, she often played hooky from school and found herself on the golf course. I suppose you could say we were all rather obsessed with it!

However proficient Lawrence and I were, Mandy played especially well, and by the age of 14 she was playing in the first-team county matches with a handicap of just four. On one occasion, however, Mandy and I had a knockout match against each other and she was finding it really difficult to concentrate on her game. She very sweetly said that she didn't feel she should be competing against me and she wasn't playing anywhere near her best. When I was winning on the third hole, I told her to forget she was playing against her mother and instead think she was playing against someone she didn't like. She eventually beat me on the 23rd hole!

We made many friends at the golf club and a lot of our social life was focused around it. My closest friend there was a woman called Sonia, whose brother had been one of the founding members of the club. Sonia and I had exactly the same sense of fun and always had a great time together. Our relationship was to become even stronger as Lawrence and I both adored the man who became her second husband, Alf Bowman. She became Lady Captain about four years before I did, and, when I was Lady Captain in 1986, Alf was the Gentleman Captain at the time.

Life was good for Lawrence and me; we had each other, our lovely daughter, masses of friends, old and new, and I imagined that it would carry on like that for ever. Just going to Dyrham every week was like a little holiday for us because we loved it so much and we didn't want for anything. We just enjoyed life with Mandy going off to school, her dancing lessons and parties, and Lawrence and I working hard and enjoying a lively social life. It was a lovely, happy time. The three of us loved being together as a family.

For me, the happiest times I have ever spent with Mandy were on the golf course and one of the greatest pleasures of my life was watching her play golf. She truly was amazing and would have become a professional had it not been for the events that were to devastate all of our lives.

CHAPTER 14

Lawrence and I had been married for around 14 years and we were just enjoying life like any other normal family when he started behaving a little out of character.

In 1971, when we were all about to go off on one of our boating holidays, I had to go away for work, so Lawrence and Mandy went without me and Mandy took a friend along with her to keep her company.

The holiday started fine and was going without a hitch, until one day when Lawrence was fastening everything off on the boat as they were mooring up. I don't know exactly what happened, but suddenly Lawrence fell over the side and into the water. Even though he was a perfectly good swimmer, he started panicking and flailing around. Mandy, meanwhile, went into a complete panic and didn't know what to do. She was 12 at the time, so she knew she needed to throw him some kind of lifeline, but it all became too much for her and she started throwing everything she could lay her hands on overboard – including, for some reason, a hairbrush!

Eventually, someone from another boat saw what was happening and was able to throw Lawrence a rope and pull him onto dry land. Later that day, I got a call from him and he told me about his fall.

Or at least he tried to tell me, but he honestly didn't know what had happened. It was just a momentary lapse of concentration, as if he had 'powered down' for a few minutes. He couldn't understand why he had reacted the way that he had as he was a confident swimmer and, really, falling overboard shouldn't have been such a big deal. But, for that one moment, he totally blanked.

We didn't think anything more about it – we just thought it was one of those glitches in life and carried on as normal. But, shortly after the boating incident, I began to notice that Lawrence was behaving differently and he started drinking more than usual. He had always liked a drink, but gradually over the space of a few months it began to look as if Lawrence was becoming quite dependent on alcohol.

We would always drink socially if we went out to dinner with friends or had people over, and enjoyed a few drinks at the weekends when we were at home together. It was never anything excessive. This, on the other hand, was much more than usual.

Lawrence and I had vowed to always be honest with each other, so, when he would reach for the bottle in the evening, I would ask him whether he'd had a particularly bad day at work, or I'd say 'let's have a nice coffee instead' and things like that. I didn't make a big deal about his drinking because at that stage it wasn't something that worried me unduly; I suppose I just wasn't used to him drinking every single night and I knew that it could be a slippery slope to a more serious problem.

But, as well as the frequency of his drinking, he seemed to be drinking much bigger measures than normal. On a couple of occasions I remember him knocking back spirits as if it was lemonade, pouring huge measures and becoming incoherent as a result.

I hated myself for doing it, but after a little while I began taking note of the levels on the bottles in the drinks cabinet. I didn't mark the bottles, I would just keep an eye on how quickly Lawrence was getting through the Scotch. It was awful feeling that I had to check up on him, but I knew it was something I had to keep an eye on. At that stage I didn't confide in anyone about my concerns. I hoped that I was wrong about my suspicions. It was all so out of character.

The trouble was, when we were out socialising, our friends encouraged Lawrence to drink because he was so much fun and uninhibited when he was merry. He was always great at telling jokes and reciting things like the RAF alphabet (which, as you will know if you've ever heard it, is very rude!). What's more, he was never aggressive when he was tipsy – just more open and relaxed. I suppose, if he had been an angry drunk, I would have done something about it more quickly.

Nevertheless, I decided to talk to my GP about it and he dismissed it with something along the lines of, 'Well, we all like the odd drink, don't we?' But, as time went on, Lawrence's concentration seemed to become very poor and he started repeating himself. We would laugh about it to start with, and I would tease him for being a bit absent-minded as I thought that was all it was. We all forget things, after all. Then, one day, he literally asked me the same question three times in a row. I looked him in the eye thinking that he would break into a smile because he was just being cheeky, but there was no reaction. I remember feeling quite cold all of a sudden.

Again, I went to see our GP and told him my concerns, but the doctor didn't think Lawrence had a problem at all. If anything, I was made to feel I was just being neurotic. He just repeated what I'd told myself – the fact that we all forget things at times. He didn't take the situation seriously at all. I told him that this was happening regularly now, not just 'at times', but the doctor said it was probably due to tiredness or stress and that I shouldn't worry about it.

So for three to four years I just let it go on and on, thinking that maybe Lawrence had just become forgetful. I suppose I convinced myself that the doctor had been right – he was a doctor, after all. And it just became the way that Lawrence was. When you get used to a situation, it quickly becomes the norm anyway. But every so often, when I was at the doctor for a check-up, I'd mention it again and he would always say the same thing, that there was nothing to worry about. I didn't want to sound like a nag.

I understood why it was difficult to think Lawrence had any kind of problem as he was still the same lovely, quiet, gentle, always smiling man everyone knew; I was the excitable one! However, it got to the stage on occasions where even the smallest amounts of alcohol seemed to affect him and his speech would become slurred. I just put it down to getting older. He was 13 years older than me and I wondered whether you just naturally aged faster as time went on.

But the changes in him became more and more obvious to me. At first, when he repeated himself, it was annoying, but then it got more serious. I remember one trip up to Scotland when Lawrence kept saying the same thing over and over again. It was just heartbreaking. He'd say things like 'Isn't it a lovely day today?' and then a minute later he'd say, 'It's a lovely day today,' and then 'What a lovely day' and 'Isn't it a lovely day?' and so on. Our friends Harold and Sybil (the couple from the 'Dorchester double cross') were in the car as they were holidaying with us. They were aware of the situation and very understanding, but it was obvious that something was definitely wrong.

Then, in 1971, Lawrence and I were out having dinner and our friend Stanley Coleman, with whom we always went on boating holidays, happened to be in the same restaurant and noticed

Lawrence behaving strangely. Lawrence hadn't touched any alcohol, but he fell asleep at the dinner table. I could see that Stanley was shocked by Lawrence's behaviour as he knew us both so well and he could see that I was very uncomfortable about it, too. I confided in him about all of the other things that had been happening. Thankfully, he agreed that something was definitely amiss. He knew that just wasn't the kind of thing that Lawrence would do.

Stanley used to go to the same GP as we did, and so he made an appointment and told the doctor his opinions on Lawrence's situation. It took his testimony to prove that Lawrence should be referred to a neurologist. I was frustrated that the doctor hadn't believed me and that he had dismissed me as some kind of neurotic housewife, but at least it meant I could try to get to the bottom of Lawrence's out-of-character incidents once and for all.

Unfortunately, Lawrence's behaviour wasn't the only thing that was on my mind at this time. My darling father's health had also started going downhill rapidly. All through his life he had always suffered badly from asthma and bronchitis and latterly he had suffered a series of minor heart attacks and mini-strokes. I had almost 'got used' to him being unwell. Throughout this time, he had continued to go to South Africa regularly in the winter months to avoid the damp months in England. But finally, on 1 April 1971, his poor heart gave out and he died at the Royal Masonic Hospital in Hammersmith in west London. The only comfort to us all was that he had lived to be over 80 and had lived a successful and happy life.

I was absolutely devastated to have to say goodbye to him and the prospect of life without him terrified me. My father had always been my mentor, my anchor, someone who I could always talk to and who would offer the right advice. He was always such a wonderful poppa to Mandy and everyone was grief stricken.

Looking back, though, I am grateful he did not have to witness Lawrence's decline as he would have been heartbroken to see the things Mandy and I had to go through as the years went on.

My father had always tried to do the very best for his family and everyone around him. He was the kind of person that, if he heard someone had a problem, his mind would start whirring about how he could help. When I married Lawrence, it had made him so proud and reassured that I was with someone who could love and support me the way that he always had. He would have hated to think about the devastating consequences of Lawrence's condition.

As the family tried to get through the loss of our dear father, something positive happened, as at last we got an appointment for Lawrence to see a well-known neurologist called Gerald Stern. I knew that my darling husband was already quite ill at this stage – and, in his heart, Lawrence knew it, too. I remember telling him that he was being referred to a neurologist for tests and he didn't object at all. He dutifully came along. I know he could see how concerned I was about him and that made him upset, but other than that he didn't really show any emotion about it. He just nodded when I told him where we were going, and he quietly let me hold his hand as we waited to see Dr Stern at the University College Hospital in London.

That day, my mother also came along with us. Since my father's death, she had been spending a lot of time with us, and she absolutely adored Lawrence.

In what has now become the norm for any kind of dementia testing, Lawrence was asked various simple questions to assess his basic mental health – who is the Prime Minister? What season is it? And so on. Tragically, poor Lawrence had trouble answering all of the questions. He got frustrated and would say, 'Oh, it's on the tip of my tongue, let me come back to that question …'

After the tests, Lawrence and I were asked to wait outside while

Dr Stern assessed the results. After what seemed like a matter of minutes, he called us back in and told us that, although Lawrence was only 51, it was likely he was suffering from pre-senile dementia (now called early onset dementia). He said that further blood tests would then be carried out to rule out any other conditions that could have an effect on his memory and concentration.

Dr Stern's diagnosis meant very little to me in terms of helping me understand what to do next. As I was to discover, there was absolutely no treatment for dementia and no medication for it. I was told that, if any trials or treatments that Lawrence could take part in were to come up, they would be in touch. I think they were particularly interested in him as he was relatively young to have been diagnosed with dementia, but other than that it was just a matter of monitoring the situation as we went along. I was told that there was no limit to how long the illness would go on, as people didn't die from this condition. Basically, he would have dementia for the rest of his life, but he wouldn't die from the disease.

Dementia was known as the 'Silent Epidemic' back then – primarily because it was the kind of condition that just festered away in the brain with no significantly obvious symptoms, and also because it just wasn't talked about. Back then, senile dementia was considered to be a factor of old age. It was just one of those slightly embarrassing parts of ageing. We all accepted that grandparents got a bit dotty and that was that.

Now, of course, so much more is known about the myriad neurological disorders and we are all so much more clued-up about illnesses and medical jargon. Thanks to the internet – maybe thanks isn't the right term! – we are now able to type symptoms into a search engine and, hey presto, we have a diagnosis, or at the very least a possible reason why A and B is happening.

At the time, the term Alzheimer's wasn't even used. I was later to discover that the symptoms of the disease were first described by a

German psychiatrist and neuropathologist called Alois Alzheimer in 1906. His research had resulted in the condition being known as Alzheimer's disease, but it didn't become a widely used term until much later. Now, of course, there are several other types of dementia, although Alzheimer's is still the most common.

As soon as Lawrence had been diagnosed, I tried to find out as much as I could about pre-senile dementia. Because it only affected the elderly, usually it seemed like something that 'just happened' and was part and parcel of the ageing process. You got old, your memory went, you got confused about things and so it went on. But my darling Lawrence was only 51, so why was it happening to him?

Being the determined – some might say downright stubborn – woman I was, I wasn't prepared to sit back and let Lawrence's condition get worse without doing something – anything – to help him. But it was going to be a few years until my research really gained momentum and before I got answers to any of my questions about this totally indiscriminate disease.

At that stage, it would have been wonderful to be able to talk to someone who was in a similar situation, to just pick up the phone and talk to a person who cared. It would have been a great help to be able to do something that would make life easier for Lawrence and it would have been an incredible support for me too. I felt so utterly helpless about the situation. I really wanted to understand the condition, but, short of poring over medical textbooks, which weren't written for the likes of me, I didn't know what to do.

CHAPTER 15

I found myself, at just 37 years of age, suddenly having to face up to the fact that my lovely, gentle husband was potentially very ill indeed, and that the happy family life that I had before might never be the same again. Being 13 years older, Lawrence had always looked after me and it had never crossed my mind that it would ever be any different. But from the day when he was diagnosed with pre-senile dementia, nothing would ever be the same again.

Shortly after he had been diagnosed, Lawrence had a couple of bumps when he was out driving our little brown van from the shop. One incident happened when he was driving Mandy. They weren't serious accidents, but it was enough of a warning for me to know something had to be done about it. I persuaded him to stop driving and luckily this wasn't a big issue for him. He knew that he was losing his grip on the situation. He had never argued about anything in life before anyway, so he just accepted the situation with his usual good grace.

His dementia didn't become obvious to outsiders straight away.

Within a couple of years, however, it was impossible not to notice and some of our friends at the golf club didn't know how to handle it when Lawrence kept repeating himself and acting strangely. Gradually, these 'friends' started avoiding him and it was difficult to get anyone to play a game of golf with him, which was heartbreaking to witness. When I was unable to play golf with him myself, I started paying the professional golfer at the club or one of the caddies to play a round with him so that he wouldn't think anything was amiss.

What made it more upsetting was that he wasn't doing anything wrong; it was just that his strange behaviour was too much for people to handle. A few very loyal friends were more understanding and could see that I was embarrassed when he would start saying the same thing over and over again, but I have to say that a lot of acquaintances just didn't want to know and drifted away.

Friends said they were unavailable to meet up, or literally started hiding behind pillars when we came into a room at the golf club so that we wouldn't approach them. I pretended to turn a blind eye to it, but it was incredibly hurtful. At times, I thought it was spineless of them not to approach us, but I suppose they were uncomfortable about the situation. I also had to keep watch on Lawrence all the time because, whenever he could, he would just wander off and start talking gibberish to absolutely anyone.

Some of our oldest friends didn't seem able to handle the situation at all. I know it must have been distressing for them as well, as they had effectively lost one of their close friends, but I couldn't help thinking that they could have just pretended things were OK. Knowing what I know now about dementia, Lawrence still would have been aware of the emotions around him. If people had been kind and understanding to his face, he would have been happier and more stimulated, so possibly unlikely to just wander off and try to talk to someone else.

I remember that Dennis the caddy master and Mr Titchmarsh the club secretary at the time were absolutely brilliant with Lawrence and took such wonderful care with him. They also tried to help me in whatever way they could, which I really appreciated. As I was to discover, being someone's carer is very different to being their wife.

At home, as time went on, more disturbing things would happen. Lawrence would say he was going off to the loo and then get lost in the house or start opening windows for no reason. Things got so bad that it wasn't just a case of Lawrence being a bit absent-minded. I began to seriously worry that he could harm himself because his concentration was all over the place and he was so forgetful. He would get dressed and put his pyjama top on with his suit trousers and his pants over his trousers, or he would go to make a cup of tea and put the kettle on the hob. I worried that he would do something awful like inadvertently set fire to the house or have an accident with the electrics.

I didn't realise that someone with dementia may also have perception problems. One white door might look exactly the same as the next white door, for example, and that's why he would get lost on the way to the bathroom. In addition, as I was later to find out, the memory slips back decades, so that someone with dementia can literally feel they are living in a different era of their life – for example a time when kettles were heated up on a hob, rather than being plugged in at the mains. Although I didn't know it at the time, Lawrence's strange behaviour was totally the norm for someone with dementia. But the fact that no two people have exactly the same symptoms made it even harder to grasp. There wasn't a precise list of 'symptoms' anywhere or advice on what to do when these seemingly random things happened.

I continued working in my shop, which was now a necessity rather than a hobby as our income depended on it. Lawrence was having a difficult time working with his brother, who had become very frustrated with the way he was behaving, so it was agreed that he should come and work with me. This was partly so that I could keep an eye on Lawrence, but also to see if it could spark a new interest for him. The customers got to know him and were lovely to him. He was such a lovely, smiley, gentle soul and he always adored children. The idea was for him to do the accounts for me, but it very quickly became obvious the arrangement wasn't going to work as he couldn't concentrate on the figures any more. Gradually, even simple tasks seemed to completely bamboozle him.

Having discussed the situation with close friends, we decided that, provided he had the right sort of help in the day-to-day running of the venture, we would buy a friend's little retail business that he was selling. I was prepared to guarantee the finances and I thought it would simplify things for Lawrence. It would be something of his own to work on – rather than working at Amanda, which was essentially my business. Unfortunately, as we very quickly found out, the business that we bought for Lawrence had a reputation for bad debt and I immediately discovered I couldn't get credit from any of the suppliers. No wonder I had been able to buy the business at such a bargain price!

To add insult to injury, the manager, who I had hoped would take on the lion's share of responsibility, obviously realised Lawrence wasn't as on top of things as he should have been and exploited the situation further. Not surprisingly, it didn't take too long before we were forced to liquidate the company.

I didn't want Lawrence to be made bankrupt, so it took me a few years to pay off the company's debts. I don't think the friend who sold me the business had ever considered what a nightmare it was going to turn out to be for me, especially as he knew Lawrence had dementia. But at the time I knew there was no point in stirring up more trouble with the friendship or taking legal action about it. Lawrence's situation was much more important. Quite honestly, I didn't have the energy to fight any more battles. In hindsight, I should have known it was a bad idea as my friend had also had a stressful time with the business, but I suppose I had been clutching at straws that it would work out. I had one very successful retail venture and I had hoped this one would be, too.

It then became a problem to work out what the next best step would be for Lawrence as it was obvious he couldn't handle responsibility. During that time, his dementia was being monitored and, on one occasion when he had a check-up, his brother Clifford said he would like to come along with us. I wanted him to understand what the situation was and that Lawrence was still capable of functioning on certain levels.

After the assessment, I pleaded with Clifford to take Lawrence back into his business to try to make Lawrence believe that he was doing something useful. I even said I would give him half of his wages if that would help. I was so desperate for things to be just as they were for Lawrence – and I suppose for myself, too. I liked the idea of us both going off to work every day and having an almost normal family life. I thought it would make a difference to Mandy to see her mum and dad working, just like anyone else's parents.

Clifford agreed to take Lawrence back into the business on the understanding that I would pay his wages, but very quickly it became obvious it wouldn't work out as Lawrence was given some very degrading jobs to do, which upset both him and me. I don't blame Clifford for doing this as he was obviously just trying to protect the company, but it felt very hurtful at the time.

I decided that I had to find some kind of day care for Lawrence so that I could continue to work at Amanda and he would be safe without me. There was no way that he could be left on his own. My friend Sonia suggested that I get in touch with the Jewish Welfare Board and I suggested to Lawrence that he could 'help out' there as a volunteer, rather than suggesting he was going there for help himself.

Of course, everyone else in the day-care centre was so much older than Lawrence, and they all loved him, because he was just such a loveable man. Every morning he was picked up from home by their caring volunteers, and brought back at the end of each day. He in turn felt that he was doing something very worthwhile and got amazing 'job satisfaction' from it.

At home, meanwhile, Lawrence was becoming incredibly agitated. He couldn't sleep – in fact, he couldn't really function 'normally' at all. As usual, Mandy was an angel about the situation. She was lovely and supportive and never once complained that the situation was unfair, or that other friends of hers were more fortunate than she was. Now I look back and realise that at the time her father was actually more like a child than a father figure to her, but, like everyone else, she adored Lawrence.

At that stage, there was absolutely no medication designed specifically for the treatment of dementia. The only thing that Lawrence was able to take was tranquillisers to calm his agitation down. But this caused its own problems as it would knock the stuffing out of him and he was very quiet and then just slept more and more. Without the tranquillisers, though, he would be babbling and disturbed. We could no longer have any kind of normal conversation; it was like looking after a child.

Meanwhile, Mandy and I had an extraordinary mother and daughter relationship. She became such a great friend, and because of Lawrence's illness we were always incredibly close. She was always completely dedicated and hands-on. She was totally unflappable, which was amazing when you think what the poor thing was going through at the time. I think she even seemed to feel it was up to her to take care of me. I remember that she used to grab my hand to cross the road – not for her own sake, but to look after me. That's just the way she was.

CHAPTER 16

Bad luck often seems to happen in threes, and so it proved for my family when, the very same year that Lawrence was diagnosed with pre-senile dementia and my father died, my sister Angela's husband Jerzy left her.

He had been having an affair with one of his colleagues at his textile business. Angela was absolutely devastated and soon after had a nervous breakdown. As a result, she spent some time in hospital, where she was given various forms of therapy, including electric shock treatment, which we were assured was a very effective treatment at the time. Following her treatment, she was diagnosed as suffering from manic depression, which has since been renamed the rather less violent-sounding bipolar. At that stage, she would need to be on lithium medication permanently to keep her moods on an even keel. It was a devastating time for her, but she was so incredibly brave throughout.

After a few more weeks in the psychiatric hospital, she was allowed to go home and quite quickly convinced herself – and all of us around her – that she had recovered from her mental glitch. She even took herself off the lithium treatment, which I believe is quite common with people who have the condition.

To the outside world, she was her old self again, dynamic and determined, but in truth she was having a terrible time trying to adjust to being on her own. Before her breakdown, she had always enjoyed painting and art, but she stopped altogether, which I felt was a great shame. She really was a great artist and had been blessed with an amazing gift. In a way, I was angry with her for just giving up painting on a whim – especially as I had been robbed of my own gift of singing. I have always felt that, if you have something special, you should try to make the most of it.

Slowly but surely, Angela tried to piece her life back together – minus her art. In fact, the only pre-breakdown activity that she really threw herself into was her golf. She became good at it and gradually she started to build a new life and career for herself.

Shortly after Angela was unwell, I went into hospital to have a minor procedure, which coincided with a move from our house in north London to a flat, which we believed would be a much more sensible option for Lawrence. I thought it would be easier to cope with Lawrence if we lived on just one level as I would always be close to him. He wouldn't be able to get lost on another floor of the house, or endanger himself by opening the windows too far and so on. The block of flats that we moved into also had a concierge who would be able to keep an eye on Lawrence if for any reason I wasn't there. But that didn't always go exactly to plan either.

We lived in this flat for eight years, during which time Lawrence got more and more forgetful and all the horrendous symptoms of dementia gradually became apparent. It got to the point where Lawrence became a real danger to himself as he started leaving the flat and roaming around the area. On one occasion, he tried to go out without any clothes on – until he was quickly stopped by the concierge and brought back into the building. I immediately got Lawrence an identity bracelet with my phone number on it, just in case it ever happened again and he got even further.

Nights were appalling as Lawrence was unable to settle and was confused about what was going on, but I always did my best to remain patient with him, even though, to be brutally honest, he sometimes drove me up the wall. I suppose dealing with lots of little children in the shop had given me plenty of practice. Even though he was exasperating, I never once lost my temper with Lawrence because I completely adored him, and I knew it wouldn't do any good anyway. Nevertheless, I had to start locking the front door when we were home together to stop him wandering out.

During the time that I was trying to cope at home, I was very lucky because occasionally I was able to get away for the odd weekend when friends and family could step in with Lawrence. It was a good outlet and made it easier for me to return with as much patience as I could muster. I realise I am incredibly lucky to have been able to afford this kind of respite, as it meant that I was able to take time out of my life and recharge my batteries. I would feel guilty while I was away, but, looking back, those occasional weekends really helped me keep a grip on everything.

The one really wonderful thing to come out of this terrible time at home while things were so difficult with Lawrence was that my relationship with Mandy became stronger and stronger. I honestly don't know how I would have coped without her. For that reason, one Sunday night in 1976 particularly sticks in my mind …

Mandy had invited some friends round for supper after they had been preparing for a big golf competition later in the week. Because her car was in the garage, she borrowed mine to take one of the boys home – even though she had only passed her driving test a month earlier and so she wasn't exactly used to a 4.2l automatic Jag! But Lawrence and I had already gone to bed, so she just grabbed the keys and off she went. Some time later, the phone rang and a neighbour said he had seen my car in a nasty accident.

The roads had been wet and she had seen the car skid, hit a tree, go through a hedge and smash into a brick wall. I immediately began screaming as I knew it was Mandy as I had heard her leaving the drive. Lawrence, seeing me in this state, also started screaming too. All hell broke loose! While I panicked and tried to work out what to do, there was a ring on the doorbell and there was Mandy, with a bandage around her head, supported by two ambulance men.

She told me that she had been in an accident and that she was on the way to the hospital. She had asked the ambulance men to go via our flat so that I didn't get too much of a shock receiving a call from the hospital – little did she know that our nerves were pretty much shot already! I then went with her to the hospital and she had to have 15 stitches in her head. She was allowed to come home, but I had to stay awake all night to check on her in case she had suffered concussion. Her friend Diana Curtis, who lived on the floor below us, had also come to the hospital with us. Diana stayed up with me all night and we played gin rummy together and kept checking in on Mandy. It was one of those nights you never forget. I don't think I have played gin rummy since. The important thing was that Mandy was absolutely fine, the stitches healed perfectly and there was no permanent damage. The car meanwhile was a write-off, but the one good thing to come out of it was I got a lovely orange Triumph Stag with the insurance money!

CHAPTER 17

In 1976, I was asked to become the Lady Captain of Dyrham Park Golf Club, which I was pleased to bits about. Although Lawrence was really not himself at the time, I still think he was very proud of me and I know it made him happy to see me smiling so much. To be honest, I really don't know how I managed to do it, as I had to be a carer for him, look after Mandy and run my business at the same time. Somehow, though, I did, and I think being made Lady Captain of such a prestigious golf club was not only an honour, but also a privilege to be able to give something back to the club for so much that we had benefited from and enjoyed over the years.

The majority of our social life wouldn't have happened without it. I was also aware that being Lady Captain helped me think about something else and take my mind off what we were going through at the time. The year passed and I must say that I enjoyed it, although at the end of it Lawrence was not well enough to come to the Lady Captain's Dance. This was very upsetting as it would have been the icing on the cake for me to have him by my side.

By 1978, Lawrence's dementia had progressed so far that he had become doubly incontinent. I knew then that the time had come for him to be in 24-hour care. I simply couldn't look after him by myself. I wasn't physically strong enough to be able to give him the kind of personal care that he needed, and mentally I was finding it a real struggle, too. I honestly felt I was losing my grip.

For months, I tried to get Lawrence into a nursing home for people with dementia, but I didn't have any luck at all. There didn't seem to be a single home that would take such a young man with the condition. They only seemed geared up for the very elderly and infirm. From my own point of view, I would have wanted to be with people of the same age in the same situation, but, as far as I knew then, Lawrence was a very unusual case.

So we struggled on at home for several months with as much support as we could from social services. Carers would come in every day to deal with Lawrence's washing and toilet needs, but, as anyone who has ever been in that kind of situation will tell you, it is never enough. There were numerous 'little accidents' that I dealt with, but I would be lying if I said it was straightforward. I didn't want to moan about it as I knew so many people have to cope with much harder situations, but very quickly I was physically and mentally shattered.

One year, instead of going away somewhere locally for a weekend, I found a private nursing home that would take Lawrence, while I went away for a short break to Israel with my good friend Pauline. I hoped it would benefit us both as it was a very good nursing home and I badly needed some sleep. While I was there, I went to the Western Wall (Wailing Wall) in Jerusalem and put a note in it praying that we would soon find the right nursing home for Lawrence.

On our return to our hotel in Tel Aviv that evening, Mandy phoned me to tell me the great news – that Lawrence had been accepted at the Jewish Home in Tottenham. It seemed like a miracle sparked from putting the note in the wall. The thing I'd hoped for most was finally going to happen and Lawrence would get the proper care that he so badly needed.

A few days after I got back, Mandy and I took Lawrence to the home, and he quickly seemed to settle in quite well. They were very caring there and I felt that he was in good hands. At last, it seemed that life could get back on some kind of even keel. Lawrence had a lovely room and there were all the facilities that he could possibly need. I could at last sleep at night knowing that he was in safe hands.

Strangely enough, the previous year I had been to see a spiritualist near Baker Street. (My mother was always very interested in spiritualism and so I suppose that's how I became curious about it. After my father died, I went to see a few different mediums, I suppose to try to 'connect' with him, but nothing had particularly struck a chord with me before.) However, when I saw this medium, I was staggered by the amount of things that she was describing that were completely accurate about my situation. She described Lawrence's illness – she knew it was something to do with his brain and she was even able to describe a weather vane, exactly like the one that was on top of the nursing home in Tottenham.

She went on to say that she never usually told people things that could upset them, but that she felt she had to tell me that I was in for another seven terrible years. After that, she said my life would change and that she saw 'tall buildings and water' for me. Her last observation didn't mean anything to me at the time, but later it would.

I knew that life wasn't suddenly going to get better as Lawrence's illness was likely to be long and progressive. After all, his mind was sick, but physically he was still strong. But at least it gave me some hope that, by the time I got to 50 years old, things would finally get better. However, for the moment, things were about to get even more trying …

One night, around a year later, I went out to dinner with a friend and when I got home Mandy told me that Ruth, a close friend of mine, had suffered a mental breakdown in Marbella. The hotel where she had been staying had summoned an ambulance and Ruth had been forcibly taken away. She'd had my number in the emergency contact section of her passport, which is why I had been called. As soon as I heard what had happened, I said I would go to Spain, and Mandy insisted that she would come, too, as she was also very fond of Ruth. We flew out the next day and went straight to the facility where she had been taken. Even though it was the middle of the night, I wanted to see her immediately, so we hired a car and headed straight there.

It was a horrific place – just how you would imagine a Dickensian lunatic asylum might look. It was approached by a very long dark driveway and looked like an enormous haunted house. We drove up to this little hut outside the building, which was manned by a caretaker, but, even though we begged to be let in to see her, he wouldn't allow us in as we didn't have any paperwork to show that we knew Ruth. Why on earth he thought we would be trying to visit someone we didn't know was beyond me, but that was that.

The following morning, we went to the British Consul to ask for his help, and he intervened on our behalf. But we then faced another problem. We discovered that Ruth was refusing to take her medication. Once the lithium had started working its way into her system, Ruth believed that she was cured and therefore didn't need any more medication. He told us that, as Ruth was refusing to take her meds, his hands were tied in how much he could do for her.

We left his office and went back to the asylum (as I'm sure that is what the place was) and, eventually, after much persuasion, Ruth was brought to see us. She looked ghastly and drugged up to the hilt. She didn't seem to recognise us at all and just wouldn't believe us when we said who we were. She was wearing a grey sack-like cardigan and trousers, and looked absolutely terrible. It was heartbreaking to see how ravaged she had become through depression.

I decided right away that we had to get Ruth out of that place and, although it took a while to convince the authorities to allow her to be released, I promised I would be personally responsible for her. Finally, they allowed us to take her back with us to her apartment. They told us firmly that, unless she agreed to take certain medication, she would not be allowed to fly home. We agreed with them, as we wouldn't have been able to handle her any other way.

Nevertheless, Ruth gave us a very hard time. She kept saying that we were plotting against her. In fact, Mandy and I did not manage to speak to each other privately at all for the next few days as one of us had to be with her at all times. It was only when I was in the bath one day and Mandy came in for a quick chat that we were able to speak. Even then, we had to run the tap in case Ruth heard anything we were talking about and started to get paranoid and panic.

While we were away, we spoke to Ruth's doctor many times, but she was convinced that it wasn't him and that we were all plotting against her. Finally, after hours of exasperating pleading, she agreed to take the medication, and we were all able to fly home. The journey back was remarkably uneventful and we took Ruth to the psychiatric home that her doctor had arranged so that she could be stabilised under his care. Finally, she was finally allowed to go and stay with her cousin a few days later.

When we got back to London, Mandy's fiancé was waiting to pick us up and I was appalled by how little interest he showed about what we had gone through. I remember thinking that he couldn't possibly be the right man for her. She made excuses for him, but I think she knew I was right. Indeed, shortly after this, they broke up.

Unfortunately for Mandy, after that she went on to have two more disastrous relationships. Looking back, my head was obviously in such a whirl that I didn't realise that she was just trying to find some kind of supportive male role in her life as she hadn't had that kind of support since the age of 12. It took her a long time to find her soulmate who wasn't simply filling a 'father figure' gap for her.

CHAPTER 18

The morning after we came back from our rescue mission in Spain, I went into my shop, and then on to visit Ruth. While I was there, I got a call from Mandy saying that the home in Tottenham where Lawrence was living had been in touch and they wanted to see me immediately. I was convinced that Lawrence had had some kind of terrible accident, so I went back to the shop to pick up Mandy and together we drove to Tottenham.

I remember it was raining and, on our way, I tried to warn Mandy that the news might not be good and that it was even possible that Daddy had died, so we should be prepared. We'd had such a traumatic time in Spain that we were in a total daze and weren't really thinking clearly at all to be honest. It was truly like living a nightmare. The rain made it doubly depressing, although the sunshine of Spain hadn't exactly been a cheerful time either.

When we arrived, the director of the care home told us that Lawrence had gone on one of his walkabouts and that they couldn't cope with him any more. He said it wasn't their policy to lock any doors and so it wasn't appropriate for Lawrence to stay there. The director said I was to make alternative arrangements for him immediately. No matter how much I tried to talk him round – or, rather, plead with him – he wouldn't make an exception.

Naturally, I was relieved that Lawrence was OK, but I was also completely thrown by what I was supposed to do. It had been so difficult to get him accepted there in the first place and, had it been possible to keep him at home, I would never have wanted him to go into a home. To have him back was going to be even more difficult because his illness was so far advanced by that stage. Besides, unless I went to work every day, we would lose everything.

Nevertheless, Mandy and I took Lawrence home with us and eventually we managed to get a place for him in another temporary private nursing home. I hated having to keep moving him around from place to place, but each time I longed for it to be the place where he would settle. I hoped he would gain some kind of quality of life in a proper caring environment, as they had much better facilities than I could possibly have at home. Plus, they were more geared up for his condition. However, yet again, the private nursing home that he was staying in ended up being a temporary solution because it was closing down.

We seemed to be being shunted from pillar to post, and each time poor Lawrence just became more agitated, upset and confused. Meanwhile, I felt really guilty because I seemed to be making the wrong decisions for him all of the time.

Thankfully, though, his next move was to be more permanent as one of the nurses at the private nursing home was friendly with one of the domiciliary psychiatrists in Barnet and they found a place for him at a home in Napsbury, near St Albans in Hertfordshire. Rather than just being a nursing home, this was a mental health facility that specialised in cases like Lawrence's.

To be honest, it was a pretty depressing and grim place with little to redeem it really, but at that stage Lawrence was going downhill very rapidly and needed to have proper care from qualified carers who knew the correct way to handle someone in his condition. We were concerned, for example, that if he had a fall we wouldn't know how to lift him, and even day-to-day things such as getting him to eat and bathing him needed to be handled properly.

The day we moved Lawrence there, Mandy and I were devastated when it came to leaving him, as it really felt like a very grim institution, but we vowed that we would visit him regularly, even though by this time he did not appear to recognise either of us. We were later to discover that, even if a person with dementia doesn't recognise you, your visit can still really help lift their morale, and that was the most important thing. So we were glad that we stayed true to our promise.

CHAPTER 19

Once Lawrence was settled at Napsbury, in 1979, I decided to write a letter to all of the national newspapers to try to raise awareness of pre-senile dementia. I wouldn't normally have done something like that, but I was so shell-shocked by what had been happening to me that I wanted to see if other people were going through similar situations. I felt sure that having someone on the end of the line who would listen and understand the kind of things I had been going through would really make a difference. I hoped that just maybe the stigma and ignorance about dementia could one day be a thing of the past.

The letter that I wrote to the press ended up being quite a long one, as I recounted how Lawrence had battled with the disease, how friends had reacted and how frustrated I was about not being able to find the right care for him. I finished the letter with a request for other people to get in touch if they were in a similar position. I had felt so isolated and I thought that I might feel better about my own situation if I could somehow help somebody who was facing the same problems. At that point, I didn't even think people would take any notice of my letter; I just felt that it was something that I had to do to try to come to terms with it myself.

Amazingly, just a couple of days later, Christine Doyle, the Medical Correspondent at the *Observer* newspaper, telephoned me to say that she had received my letter and that she had been very moved by Lawrence's story. She said she wanted to come and interview Mandy and me rather than just printing my letter. So she came over and spent an afternoon with the two of us. We told her the whole story, showing her pictures and sharing happy and sad memories. The experience was very cathartic for both of us. Little did we know that her piece was going to be such a huge story in the following Sunday's paper.

On 5 December 1979, I opened the newspaper and couldn't believe my eyes. Other papers had printed my letter, but this was a three-quarters-of-a-page article with pictures of myself and Lawrence. The piece was called 'The Sad Quiet Epidemic'. It was a wonderfully written article and I was very grateful that Christine had handled our story so sensitively. Yet, even in my wildest dreams, I would never have expected what happened next ...

I had hoped that possibly I would receive a letter or two from people who were in a similar situation to me, living with someone with pre-senile dementia, but I never expected the response that it would generate. Within a few days, I started to receive sacks full of mail, which were sent on to me via the newspaper.

One of the letters was from a lady in Kent called Cora Phillips whose husband had died 10 years after being diagnosed with pre-senile dementia. She told me that she had started to organise a support group dedicated to dementia and had also registered the group as a charity. It didn't have a proper name at the time and was very much in its fledgling stages. Three years earlier, she had heard a radio programme about Alzheimer's disease by Professor A.N.

Davison, which had prompted her to write to him with the idea of forming a society.

With Professor Davison's encouragement, Cora contacted several eminent experts in the field, including Dr Gordon Wilcock, a consultant physician at the Radcliffe Infirmary in Oxford, who was also researching into the disease. Professor Davison and Dr Wilcock then met with Cora and together they drew up a constitution for a new support group and registered a charity.

The aims of the proposed group were to give support to families by linking up with each other through membership. They also hoped to provide relevant literature about the illness for those affected and their carers. Another aim was to help with any social services queries. They wanted to ensure enough help was available when a patient became bedridden. At this stage, there were very few places for this type of speechless, helplessly ill patient, as I knew only too well.

The society also aimed to promote the research and education of the general public and professionals into the nature of the illness, via the press, media and fundraising.

It was astounding to see their aims on paper as, finally, there seemed to be something positive happening for dementia sufferers.

When Lawrence had been ill for a couple of years, I had looked into starting up my own support group with Dr Stern, the neurologist who had originally seen Lawrence, and some other experts in the field. I had even gone so far as to try to generate some funding. But when I read Cora's letter, it was a light-bulb moment that we should get together. It seemed fated that we were to meet and I quickly got in touch with Cora. We arranged to get together a week or so later in Surrey, where she was based.

Virtually as soon as the meeting had started, I knew that we should all focus our attention on a joint society, as it would be silly to have two groups that were essentially working towards similar goals. There and then we formed a group with Professor Gordon Wilcock as the chairman of trustees; Cora Phillips was his deputy and I was to be the honorary secretary, also in charge of public relations and fundraising.

We decided to call the charity The Alzheimer's Disease Society. At first, we were worried if it was the right name, as so few people had heard the name Alzheimer's. But that was one of our key challenges – to get more awareness for this 'silent epidemic'. We thought that having a specific name for the condition was actually a bonus, as it would hopefully prompt more interest than an umbrella term like dementia might. Dementia then – and to some extent still – means memory loss to a lot of people, but there is much more to the condition than just being forgetful.

I set to it, putting together some information and sending letters to every local newspaper in the country. Using the contacts I made through local papers, I got in touch with other support groups and started to organise fundraising events. On 13 September 1980, we had our first AGM and 98 members and friends came to the meeting, which was presided over by Professor Davison and Dr Wilcock. It felt very official and I felt positive for the first time in a long while.

At that first meeting, I read a letter I had received from Sir George Young from the Department of Health in which he offered his encouragement to the society and pledged his continuing interest. I also was able to announce that we already had 370 members. That same year, Sir Jonathan Miller became president of the society. Things were moving fast, and I couldn't have been more delighted.

All this in just one year from a simple letter to a newspaper. Of course, it was to take a great many years and tireless work from a great many individuals for The Alzheimer's Disease Society to become what it is today. At the time, though, it started to help me make sense of my own situation and my ongoing life with Lawrence. At least now I could channel my emotions about the disease into trying to do something that could really help people.

CHAPTER 20

While the wheels were in motion for the new Alzheimer's Disease Society (which was later to change its name to Alzheimer's Society), Mandy and I continued to visit Lawrence regularly at Napsbury Hospital, and we were both reassured about the care that he was receiving. It was wonderful to see them being so kind to him, but that was probably because Lawrence was such a gentle person, too. He would never have wanted to cause a fuss or be a burden to anyone. They could see the sort of person he had been and he was very easy for them to handle.

It was heartbreaking to see this lovely man, whom I had fallen in love with, married and lived with so happily, turn into someone so completely different, unable to recognise or have a conversation with either of us. It was impossible to believe that the dashing man who had followed me to Cattolica all those years earlier and won my heart with his selfless personality had become this shell of a man. All those dreams that we had shared about growing old together had been lost. It was devastating.

I knew I had lost the man I'd once known and that the special bond between us had gone. I would chat to him in the same way that I always had, but his mumbled replies had no meaning. It was soul-destroying. I used to visit him about four times a week for around an hour-and-a-half each time. I would feed him and tell him my news, though, if I'm being honest with myself, it was as much for my benefit as for his. I wanted to feel needed, when in truth he didn't need me at all.

He would just look at me blankly. I'd ask myself, 'How can this be my husband?' I loved him, but I wouldn't be being honest if I said it was the same. He would smile, but I knew that he didn't recognise me, even if I would kid myself that he did. Half of me was in denial, but even at that stage I was mourning the man I'd lost, even though he was still alive.

It was an unbelievably emotional period of my life, as, shortly after Lawrence had moved out of our home, my darling mother became very ill. She had never been a complainer, but, in the summer of 1978, she started telling us that her tummy was getting big. She was one of those people who didn't 'do' illness – her generation just got on with things like that. She had faced so many upheavals with the war and other difficult times over the years, so for her to complain about anything was quite unusual. In the whole of her life, I never remember seeing her take even a single painkiller.

The trouble was, by the time she went to see her doctor about her tummy problem, it was too late to do anything about it. She had lived very independently in Hove after my father died and, after she had eventually been to see a specialist, he telephoned my sister and asked to see us both. We knew from that moment on that it must be really serious because he had never summoned us to visit him like that before.

Angela and I drove over to see him in Hove and the doctor

explained that my mother had ovarian cancer. He said it was so advanced that there was little that could be done. Without any kind of treatment, he said, she would probably live for about another six months, but that she would be in a lot of pain and would need constant care. The alternative, he told us, was that she could have an operation to remove the cancerous growth. He was very frank with us and told us that the operation could spread the cancer around the rest of her body, causing her to die even more quickly.

Having spent the last few years watching Lawrence slip away from me, the idea that my mother was going to suffer was just too hideous. Mummy was incredibly independent and would never have entertained the idea that someone would have to bathe, feed and care for her in her dying days. She had always told us that we must never let that happen.

Angela and I discussed the situation with Mummy, telling her that, if she didn't have the operation, she would have to move in with either myself or Angela, but she hated that idea. She didn't want to be a burden on anyone. She was adamant that she would have the surgery, whatever the risks. After all, there was a slim chance that, once the growth had been removed, she might recover. At 71, she had had a long and vibrant life and she wasn't about to just lie down and let the cancer slowly kill her. Her mind was made up and she was going to have the surgery.

I was totally distraught about her decision. But after all that had happened with Lawrence and the fact I had a full-time job and was heavily involved in my work with The Alzheimer's Disease Society, to be really honest, I knew it would be difficult to care for her as well if she had chosen the option to end her days with one of us.

In the end, it was a very easy decision to make – and she made it. She said she would have the operation and we would let fate take its course. She was not the sort of person who could conceive living out the rest of her days in pain. It may sound callous that we didn't insist that she moved in with us to try to make the most of her last months – after all, we knew in all likelihood that the operation wouldn't be an end to her cancer – but it was her decision to make, not ours. In the same way that we wouldn't want someone telling us how to live our lives, we weren't about to tell her how to end hers.

When I saw Mummy before her operation in September 1978, I knew that in all likelihood it would be the last time that I would ever see her. But it was an unspoken goodbye between us. As I say, she didn't 'do' illness. Sure enough, two days after my darling mother's operation to remove the cancer, she silently slipped away. She never regained consciousness after the operation as the cancer had indeed rampaged through her system, just as the surgeon had warned us that it might.

It was heartbreaking, but in a way it had been the sensible thing to let her call time on her suffering. Having been through the horrific experience of seeing Lawrence going from a healthy happy man in his prime to just dwindling away slowly, in the same situation I believe we would all choose to die as quickly and painlessly as possible. It may sound cold, but, unless you have been through a kind of living death with someone whom you completely adore, it is difficult to understand. It wasn't a decision we had made easily; all of the family was involved and in agreement, but ultimately it was Mummy's choice.

Mummy's body was brought back to London and she was buried near my father in Willesden in north London. I remember her shiva (wake) vividly. I was heartbroken – not just about my mother's death but also for my 'loss' of Lawrence. The gathering was held in my flat, so I had pictures of him everywhere, and, when friends came over for evening prayers, we found ourselves facing a large portrait of the two of us. It was incredibly emotional and one of my friends explained to the rabbi why I was so distraught.

About a week later, when the official mourning period, the shiva, was over, the rabbi asked me to visit him. While I was there, he wanted me to promise that I would divorce Lawrence. I can't remember exactly what he said the reason was, but when he saw me he said, as I was still relatively young, I 'wouldn't be fulfilling myself as a Jewish woman' unless I divorced him. Of course I knew at that time that I wasn't able to have any more children and I think he would have known this, too, but, for whatever reason, he said I needed to seek a divorce. I think his motives were for the best, but I remember being horrified that he would even suggest it. I still adored Lawrence and I never even entertained the idea. I never considered that I'd marry again.

As time went on with Lawrence, though, I wondered how much longer I would see this shell of a man with no quality of life just existing. At one point, I remember holding a pillow near his face and thinking about doing the unthinkable as I just couldn't take any more. Seeing him like that for seven years while he was in nursing homes – the culmination of a 20-year illness – felt like an eternity.

Lawrence was to be at the home in Napsbury for eight years, and, although he was cared for beautifully, he went from being a lovely-looking healthy man to four-and-a-half stone and a shadow of his former self. At this stage in my life, I really felt as if I was widowed already as I was living the life of a single person. While I hadn't thought about starting a new relationship while Lawrence was alive, the physical side of our marriage had been over for many years. I felt very much alone.

My relationship with Mandy was wonderful, thank heavens. I know that her teenage years had been very difficult in terms of not having a father figure – and this was to blight her own relationships later on – but we had an incredible bond between us. When we were working in the shop together, people would say that we were like a double act and, yes, we were a great team. She was always so gregarious and chatty, it was as if she had been born confident.

I, meanwhile, prided myself on running the business as cleverly as I could. I always worked on getting the best discounts possible by paying bills early and regularly negotiated with suppliers. I got a real kick out of it, and it helped give a balance to my life. Professionally, I was totally in control, but personally there was always the sadness of my darling Lawrence.

Quite honestly, I don't know how I would have got through this time without Mandy and our network of incredible friends. And, as things slowly worsened, we had more and more support from our dear friend Micky Yager. Like so many of our circle, Lawrence and I met him and his wife Lyta at the golf club, and Lyta and I became great friends. There was quite an age gap between Lyta and Micky but they had been married for many years and were in business together. Not only were they our friends, but they also became really fond of Mandy – and even a bit possessive of her as they had no children of their own. Later, when they split up, Mandy and I became closer to Micky – he was like a brother to me and an uncle to Mandy. He was always so generous and he gave Mandy a little Yorkshire terrier for her 21st birthday, which she called Benson, after the character on television; he also gave Mandy away at her wedding. He was always such a tower of strength to both of us and so generous with his time and money. He was a wonderful support to us, especially while Lawrence was in Napsbury.

CHAPTER 21

I tried to make the best of my life for the sake of my own sanity and Mandy's happiness. I also threw myself into everything I could possibly do for the Alzheimer's Society. As it was a totally new venture, we were sort of making it up as we went along, trying things out, writing lots of letters and seeing what feedback we got and so on.

The Alzheimer's Society now has wonderful premises in London, but to begin with we had our general meetings at the National Hospital in Queen Square in London, while our awareness and fundraising meetings were held at the Nightingale Home in south London.

It was at one of these meetings at Nightingale that we decided that it was time to produce a newsletter to let members know what was going on. We knew that the only way a venture like this would ever really be successful was to involve as many people as possible, hence the newsletter. As no one felt able to be the editor, it fell upon me as secretary to take up the role. Oh boy, my English teacher at school would have been killing herself with laughter if she had ever thought I would go on to tackle something like that. Nevertheless, I tried my best and the first newsletter was sent out in January 1981. It had the necessary information, but I have to admit it was very amateurish. Better than nothing, though, I suppose.

To kick off the newsletter, I congratulated our then chairman, Dr Gordon Wilcock, on receiving a research fellowship from the Royal College of Physicians to expand his research interests in Alzheimer's disease. I then asked for volunteers to become area secretaries so that we could get local groups started. If we had a much bigger framework, we could work together to improve the conditions for people with dementia and their carers.

Whereas a lot of work with the Alzheimer's Society is for the people who live with dementia, my own experiences of being a carer had taught me how vital it was to support their carers, too. Their needs are just as great as the person in their charge.

That same year, I received a call from the BBC asking if it would be possible for the presenter Roy Hudd to interview Cora Phillips and me on his BBC1 programme *The 60 70 80 Show*. As it sounds, it was a programme aimed at older people and covered all sorts of subjects that affected the over-sixties. I spoke to Cora and we agreed that we would be delighted to be able to spread the word on television. The next thing I did was buy a suit and book a facial. The show was a great success and many new members were recruited because of it. It was a fantastic platform for the Alzheimer's Society, even though it had been thoroughly nerve-racking at the time. Me on TV, who would have thought it!

After growing up in such a charity-driven family, I found it easy to organise fundraising events. It was a buzz to start off with nothing and eventually pull off a successful project. For some reason, I have always been good at persuading people to offer their time and money; it has held me in good stead all my life. My friends probably see me coming now and think, 'Oh dear, what's she going to ask for this time?' But I have so many dear friends who have continued to support my various ventures over the years.

In 1983, I started to organise a fundraising golf tournament at Dyrham Park, which has since become an annual event. For the price of a ticket, there would be brunch, a day of golf, a cocktail party, raffles and fundraising auctions, plus a dinner and a prize-giving session. I chose Dyrham Park as, even though things hadn't been wonderful there for me and Lawrence before he was diagnosed, I still had many friends there who were willing to support my endeavours for the society. Besides, it's an incredible golf course, so it was the perfect location.

CHAPTER 22

It was through this first golf event that I approached a wonderful man called Gerald Kayman to participate in the event and also act as one of the sponsors. Gerald was a member of nearby Hartsbourne Golf Club. We had known each other for years through other friends, and I had always thought he was a very impressive person. He was one of those people who was instantly likeable; he had so much charisma without ever being the least bit arrogant or showy. He was tall, dark and handsome and incredibly well respected by everyone who knew him.

I had written to everyone I knew who might have been in the position to act as a sponsor for the golf event, so it wasn't as if I just made a beeline for Gerald, but I suppose that somewhere in the back of my mind I was thinking that maybe it would be nice to get to know him a bit better.

I duly sent off my letter and the next time I saw Gerald socially we chatted and – OK, I admit it – we had a little flirt. He was in the process of getting a divorce from his wife of many years. They were still amicable, but the marriage had been over for a long time. Talking to him, I realised that it was the first time in a long while that I had felt attractive and it was lovely. Within a day or so, he phoned me about the event, and in his inimitable way he asked me if I was 'available for feeding'.

I knew that this was going to be a date, and under normal circumstances I would never have agreed to lunch with another man while I was still married. But my circumstances weren't normal. I still loved Lawrence dearly and would always do my best for him, but, even with lots of support around me, I felt very alone and it was good to feel butterflies again. I decided that I should throw caution to the wind and agreed to meet up with him.

A few days later, I found myself having dinner in the centre of London at a restaurant called Sale e Pepe. It was a wonderful evening, and Gerald and I seemed to have so much to talk about. We had known each other casually for years at this stage so we had a lot in common. He loved the fact that I was a businesswoman and had made such a success of my shop, and he was very interested in all the work that I was doing with the Alzheimer's Society.

We talked and talked, and by the time the evening was over I think I had made up my mind that he was absolutely marvellous. My heart was racing when we said goodbye. What was so lovely was I think he felt the same way. It was wonderful. It was exciting. It was what I had missed for so many years.

I had put all of my cards on the table and was completely honest with Gerald. He knew that Lawrence was in a home and that I was still as married to him as I could be. Gerald had also known Lawrence socially before he became ill and he was incredibly sympathetic about our life together. He knew that I was in an impossibly difficult situation, and he certainly didn't rush me into any kind of relationship. But, after that first evening, we knew there would be many more dates to come.

By this stage, Lawrence wasn't communicating in any way at all. There seemed to be no life behind his eyes. I took Gerald with me on one of my visits and he was wonderful with him. I felt so lucky to have a friend like him and, while I know it could have seemed like an awkward situation having my 'boyfriend' and my husband in the same place, it really wasn't like that at all. Lawrence was an adult man who was becoming a child. Gerald was a very fine human being who was trying to support me.

Mandy, meanwhile, was delighted for me that I was finding love again with Gerald. She was 24 by then and had experienced her own share of heartache, so she was very pragmatic about my life and understood the whole situation. She would never have wanted me to be alone for ever so she was happy that Gerald was there for me. The two of them got on really well. It was lovely for her to be able to have a strong male physical presence in her life again, especially someone who was so dependable.

While I did my usual thing of charging around with the shop, going to Alzheimer's Society meetings, visiting Lawrence and trying to run the home, Gerald was there to support us both. It was so reassuring to have a sturdy frame around us again. Gerald had two children of his own and had no problem in bonding with Mandy and treating her as if she was his own daughter. The whole situation felt incredibly secure and solid.

Not long into our relationship Gerald took me away to Mombasa in Kenya, which was just fantastic. We were away for a fortnight, with a four-day safari in the middle of the holiday. We stayed in the most amazing hotel, which I remember had a bar in the middle of the swimming pool. It was so luxurious. This kind of lifestyle was so intoxicating after what I had been through in the past few years with Lawrence. I was swept up in happiness.

A few days after arriving in Kenya, we were picked up by taxi to join up with the other people who were going on safari. As we met up with the others, all of a sudden I heard, 'Morella, I don't believe it!', and there were my lovely young friends Debbie and Stephen, whom I had met at a hotel when I'd had a respite weekend from Lawrence. They were on their honeymoon and were also going on safari. The four of us had a great time together. The big animals were fantastic, but we could have lived without the little creepy-crawly ones. The holiday was absolutely a laugh a minute. The really lovely thing was that Debbie fell pregnant on her honeymoon, and she and Stephen honoured me by making me their child Zara's godmother. It's hard to believe that Zara now has a child of her own.

CHAPTER 23

It seemed almost inevitable that, within a month of Gerald and I seeing each other, our relationship became serious. This didn't mean I spent any less time with Lawrence. If anything, I spent more time with him, as Gerald would often drive me over to Napsbury to the care home. He would then either wait in the car while I went to see Lawrence, or come in with me and we would chat with Lawrence together.

A couple of months after our first date, I moved into Gerald's apartment in St John's Wood. Our friends were thrilled for us and totally understood the situation. After all, it wasn't as if the moment that Lawrence had become ill I had dated the first man that came along. It had been several years of heartache.

I realise in writing this it appears as though I am constantly trying to justify my actions, but, although it seems like it was a very short space of time between our starting to see each other romantically and moving in together, there was a lot of soul-searching about whether I was doing the right thing. Fortunately, I had the blessing of everyone around me.

Our friends even helped us throw a 'Getting Together' party. I remember being over the moon at the party and finally, finally, really happy again. I was 49 years old – soon to be 50. But I felt like I had a new chance of happiness. With Gerald, our time together felt like one wonderful event after another and we were blissfully happy together. He wouldn't allow me to feel guilty about Lawrence, as I was doing my utmost for him.

One weekend, Gerald took me away to a lovely hotel in the Cotswolds for a weekend and we started discussing how we could celebrate my 50th birthday. Sheepishly, I told him that I would really like to go to Paris, but he said, 'We can do better than that, let's go to New York!'

Little did I know that we would be flying the morning after a wonderful surprise party that my daughter had secretly been planning for me. Gerald arranged the most fabulous trip for the two of us and we had the time of our lives, staying at a wonderful hotel, shopping on Fifth Avenue, seeing shows on Broadway and visiting Central Park and all the famous landmarks. 'Tall buildings, and water', just as the medium had once told me …

Life was wonderful. As well as being a well-respected goldsmith by trade, Gerald was also a magistrate, which he loved. He was known for his ability to always see every side to a situation and was a very solid thinker. He was the kind of person that, if you were at a dinner party, he would wait until everyone had given their opinion, then he would suggest a different perspective to the situation. He would often say, 'Have you considered this …', really engaging people to challenge their own opinions. He would keep conversation alive.

Two other great friends of ours from the golf club were Teri and Ernie Bernberg, who were known as the 'beautiful couple' because they were so good-looking. Gerald and Ernie hit it off straight away, as did Teri and myself and we had many lovely times together. He was very dapper, with an amazing shock of fabulous grey hair, and she was a beautiful blonde. It was their second marriage and they obviously adored each other. Together with Gerald, Teri and Ernie joined my ADGS (Alzheimer's Disease Golf Committee), and Ernie was more than generous, not only with his money but also with the amount of time that he devoted to the charity. The four of us had some wonderful holidays together, including one when we went to Ireland and played various courses, mainly in the rain! I won an Irish £5 note from Ernie, which I still have and treasure.

Gerald and I had a fantastic friendship and a great social life, surrounded by wonderful friends. We had a marvellous time and both worked very hard. Gerald represented Great Britain at several international jewellery fairs in his role as the president of the British Giftware Association, and occasionally I would accompany him, which felt very glamorous at the time. We went to conferences in Italy, Austria and Switzerland. It was very special, not only to visit these beautiful places but also to go away with someone whom I now loved so completely. Gerald had put the spark back in my life. At 50, I still felt pretty young!

When it came close to Gerald's 60th birthday, I racked my brains as to how we could celebrate it. I love organising surprises – maybe even more than receiving them – and decided on a surprise trip to Paris on the Orient Express. I secretly packed suitcases for the two of us and got Mandy to wait for us on the station platform. Come the morning of his birthday, Gerald was really grumpy, as he hated not knowing what was going on, but he was quite happy when he saw the limo waiting to take us to the station. As we got closer to the station, he kept saying, 'Are we going to Brighton?' as he was convinced that was where we were going until he saw Mandy on the platform for the Orient Express. He was absolutely thrilled to bits by the surprise and there was more to come. I'd booked a suite in a hotel off the Champs Elysées and arranged for Mandy, Gerald's son Martin and his daughter Shelley, and all of their partners, to join us for a surprise meal for him in the hotel restaurant. He was absolutely stunned when he saw everyone waiting to celebrate with him. The whole thing was fabulous and a great treat for both of us.

CHAPTER 24

Back in London, life ticked over as before, with both of us working, enjoying our social lives and continuing to see Lawrence. Yes, in theory, I could have kept a bedside vigil with Lawrence, but at that stage he didn't even know I existed. Alzheimer's had taken over his mind and body, and what I was doing with my life had absolutely no effect on his. He was being cared for in the best way available. He was safe, fed and as comfortable as possible.

Lawrence and I were no longer married in the conventional sense of living as man and wife, and I began thinking about what the rabbi had said to me shortly after my mother died about divorcing Lawrence. I started to think that maybe I should consider marrying again. Of course, at this stage, it was too late to get a Jewish divorce (known as a 'Get'), as Lawrence would have had to agree to it and he wasn't of sound mind. In hindsight, I should have thought more about obtaining a Jewish divorce earlier, but I didn't at the time as I saw no reason to. However, I knew that legally I could apply for a standard divorce, which would mean I would be able to marry Gerald.

Physically, Lawrence and I were completely estranged, but my relationship with Gerald was becoming stronger and stronger. Once, when I was at a trade show in London, I was talking to a sales rep on one of the stands and picking out a tie for Gerald. When he asked me who I was buying it for, my first reaction was to say 'My husband Gerald', even though we weren't married. Something clicked and I thought to myself, 'Will the real Morella Fisher please stand up.' I knew that the time had come to divorce Lawrence.

For me, this decision didn't mean that I was suddenly going to stop seeing Lawrence, or think of him as anything other than my husband. As far as I was concerned, the divorce was just a piece of paper. By this time, Lawrence had been in Napsbury psychiatric home for three years and wasn't communicating in any way. So when the day came and the divorce came through in 1984 it wasn't a particularly momentous event and there were no tears. I would still always love Lawrence and I continued to visit him and care for him as much as I could. It just meant that life could move on for me with Gerald.

CHAPTER 25

Stirred on by what I had gone through with Lawrence, I continued my efforts to help awareness and fundraising for Alzheimer's. Initially, I did all the work from Mandy's old bedroom at home. Two or three years down the line, we were to move to much bigger offices in Fulham and began employing staff. It still wasn't exactly luxurious as the office was up three flights of rickety stairs, but at least we were moving in the right direction.

After the incredible feedback I had received following Christine Doyle's piece in the *Observer*, things had quietened down as far as newspaper coverage was concerned. Alzheimer's wasn't one of those diseases that people really wanted to talk about and a lot of the time the issue was just swept under the carpet. Not like today, when there is a headline about Alzheimer's disease and supposed cures for the condition practically every day.

One thing that did help raise awareness was an article that appeared in one of the papers about the glamorous 1940s actress Rita Hayworth. People had assumed that she was suffering from alcoholism, but it was revealed that she too had Alzheimer's. The fact that this beautiful and vibrant actress had also been struck down by this cruel disease helped underline the fact that Alzheimer's wasn't just something that affected the very old and infirm. It was terrible news, but it helped spark new interest in the subject.

As awareness began to gain momentum again, I was able to set up some great fundraising events. The wife of the MP Greville Janner used to come into my shop, so I wrote to Greville and told him about our endeavours. He wrote straight back to me and kindly arranged a tiddlywinks event between the Conservative Party and Oxford University. It was lovely that people were prepared to put their serious thinking brains into something as fun as tiddlywinks.

Another night, I ran a film special to raise funds and somehow managed to get Jack Lemmon to attend. I wasn't connected with any celebrities, it's just that a friend of a friend knew that he was going to be in London at the time and, as it was a charity venture, he agreed to come along. It was a great coup for the society. On another occasion, through various connections, we were able to get the singer Frankie Vaughan to appear at one of our musical fundraisers. I also hosted a cocktail party at the Martini Terrace in Haymarket in London at which the former Prime Minister John Major was the guest of honour. It was all just a matter of identifying opportunities and making the most of contacts, which was something I seemed to be quite good at.

None of this happened overnight, of course, and a lot of the time was spent sending out letters. I used to try to do a bit every day before I went to work in the shop and then a bit more when I got home in the evening. Meanwhile, I would visit Lawrence two or three times a week and spend quality time with Gerald and Mandy, so it was a very busy and fulfilled period of my life.

Gerald and I had a wonderful life together – lots of friends, a fabulous social life, it was all just marvellous. Mandy adored him and there was never any awkwardness about Lawrence. So, when we announced that we were going to get married in 1986, like everyone around us, Mandy was delighted.

That day, Gerald had left home in the morning at 7am as usual to go to work so that he could then go on to be at the magistrates' court by 10am. This particular morning, he nipped home between work and court and I remember him coming into the lounge, getting down on one knee and, with ring in hand, asking me to marry him. Needless to say, I said, 'Yes please!' and off he went to do his session in court. It was as simple as that.

As I had been unable to get a Jewish divorce from Lawrence, it meant that we couldn't marry in an orthodox synagogue, so Gerald contacted his rabbi to say he would be leaving the synagogue so that he could marry me. He explained the predicament he was in and told the rabbi that, while he would very much have liked to continue his membership, he was unable to do so.

The rabbi then surprised Gerald by trying to talk him into staying on, telling him that, if we got married in a registry office, I could then join the synagogue, too. This sounded great, but then he told Gerald that, in order for this to happen, he would have to charge us double the usual amount of fees. Gerald wasted no time telling him what he felt about his proposal, saying he couldn't live a lie and didn't want his future wife to be seen as some kind of second-class citizen in the synagogue. It was upsetting for Gerald as he had been a member of the same synagogue all of his life, but he couldn't countenance that level of double standards. 'Yes, your new wife is welcome to join us, but it will cost …'

We decided on a smallish wedding on (lucky) Tuesday, 29 July 1986. We kicked off the day with drinks at our flat for around 30 guests. Jacques, of Gill y Jacques in Charlbert Street, London, made my outfit and joined us for drinks, as did my lovely hairdresser Janet. We then all piled on to an open-top double-decker bus we'd hired for the day, which took us to Marylebone Registry Office in London. Thankfully, it was a beautiful day and we were all in such a good mood and were waving from the bus to everyone in the street that we passed!

At the registry office – the same one that my parents had married at all those years before and where I had married Lawrence – we had a basic ceremony, although to me there was absolutely nothing basic about the occasion. It was just that we chose a simple service with standard vows and legalities. The whole thing only took about 20 minutes, but it was the rest of the day that we were all really looking forward to. Our bus then picked us up and took us on to The White Elephant restaurant in Curzon Street in Mayfair, where we had the most wonderful lunch with our close friends and family. It was all very over-the-top and lavish, but we enjoyed every minute of it. Before the evening celebrations, we went back home for a little rest and a cup of tea, then headed off to Dyrham, where we had an even more lavish party for around 120 guests.

I remember that we couldn't decide how to plan the tables and didn't want to have the usual top table with the family and everyone else on 'less important' tables, so we just had a little table for two and joined everyone else during the course of the evening. When we arrived at the reception, two teddy bears were sitting in our seats, dressed as a bride and groom.

The whole evening was perfect. Mandy made a fabulous speech, joking about how Gerald had rung her to ask her for my hand in marriage and she had only consented after much deliberation. I still have her notes from that day. One part in particular has stayed with me: 'I'm very proud of my mother and this is certainly one of the greatest days of my life, to see her married to Gerald and both of them looking so happy. Not only has Mummy gained a husband, I feel I have gained the love from Gerald of a father. I even get 50p pocket money!'

It was so wonderful that she was so happy about the situation after all that we had been through together. It really was the most magical day and I felt truly happy at long last.

The following day, we went off to watch the horseracing at Goodwood. Gerald's accountant had a box there so we were really spoiled. Then we jetted off to Spain for our honeymoon. Flying had come a long way since my honeymoon with Lawrence and I had got over my collywobbles. While we were there, Gerald decided his wedding present would be a flat and holiday home in Puerto de la Duquesa. We saw the plans of one that was being built and he bought it there and then. It was to be the first of several homes that I have had in Spain as I love the place – and especially the weather!

Back home, life with Gerald was lovely. I was still working hard in the shop and Mandy was working there with me – along with her lovely Yorkshire terrier Benson, who would sit in the window of the shop and became quite a star. Children would come in to see the dog and worry if he wasn't there! He was such a sweet little thing. One time when I had to have a minor surgical procedure he sat by me the whole time I was convalescing.

Gerald loved the fact that I had my own thriving business and he never suggested that I give it up and become the dutiful housewife. I have never been that kind of person anyway. He knew that it gave me such a buzz to have my work in Amanda and do my work for the Alzheimer's Society. And he was wonderful about Lawrence. Gerald knew I would always love Lawrence and was committed to looking after him. I suppose he knew my life was difficult enough without his putting extra pressures on me.

CHAPTER 26

On Tuesday, 23 February 1987, my darling Lawrence finally passed away, aged 67. In his final year, he had developed pneumonia, which is something that often affects people who have Alzheimer's as their swallowing becomes more difficult. Some people say it is a blessing because the quality of life is so low at this point.

Being the fighter that he was, Lawrence managed to recover from his first bout of pneumonia, but the second time, as he was so much weaker and with his mind totally controlled by Alzheimer's, there just wasn't any of him left to fight back. Just as quietly and gently as he had lived life, he softly slipped away.

Sadly, I wasn't with him at the time. I'd had a phone call from the home that his health was rapidly deteriorating and I had tried to get there in time to hold his hand and be with him at the end, but I didn't make it. Mandy and I would have loved to have been with him, but at least we could take solace in the fact that we had said our goodbyes previously on two occasions. Because of his illness, I think we had both started the process of mourning a long time before his actual death.

I would be lying if I said I didn't find some kind of release when Lawrence finally died. But I know it was a release for him, too. What kind of quality of life was he enduring? He had been taken over by this cruel disease and all that was left was a husk of a magnificent man. I am certain that, if Lawrence had been able to put his feelings into words, he wouldn't have wanted to carry on existing like that.

Yes, I felt relief on my part. If things had been different and he hadn't been a victim of this tragic illness, I would have been totally devastated to lose him. The sadness came from thinking what our lives could have been like. How lovely it would have been to grow old together as a family and for him to have lived to see Mandy's beautiful children. But it was a happy-ever-after story that was never meant to be.

CHAPTER 27

On the day of Lawrence's funeral, family and friends met at Mandy's flat before making their way to the cemetery. There were many friends at the cemetery and several of them recounted happy memories of Lawrence before his illness. It felt so strange, almost as if they were talking about someone else. To me, it felt somehow as if 'my' Lawrence had died many years before.

At least, I suppose, I could take some comfort in knowing that I had tried to help other people living with Alzheimer's. At the time of writing, we are still nowhere near a cure for the disease, but so much more is known about the condition and there seems to be a genuine commitment from the government to move research forward. I think it is unlikely to happen in my lifetime, but I am confident that one day there will be a way of eradicating this vile disease.

Only a few days after Lawrence's funeral, I had to click back into businesswoman mode. It was the buying season, the time of year when I had to select the new stock for the shop, and which meant heading off to Italy for an exhibition. Travelling there gave me the breathing space I needed to take stock of my life. Choosing new things and breathing new life into the shop with a new collection also gave me an opportunity to think about life going forward for myself.

Daily life carried on much as it had before. I found that I missed those times visiting Lawrence, even though they were quite empty visits in the great scheme of things, but life had to move on. It was a cruel existence for Lawrence to have continued to endure. Gerald and I were working hard at our day jobs and with fundraising events. We also still played lots of golf and went away to our lovely flat in Spain. Because Lawrence had never been part of my life when I was in Spain, I think I felt the most relaxed I had ever been when I was there with Gerald. Home life was great, and I could almost breathe a sigh of relief that things could get back on to an even keel.

Then, yet again, fate was about to deal another cruel hand.

CHAPTER 28

The year after Lawrence died, Gerald mentioned that he had 'a bit of tummy trouble'. Like my mother, Gerald was never one to mention if he felt unwell, so the fact that he had said anything at all should have rung loud alarm bells. Unbeknown to me, he had already been to see his doctor, who had referred him to a specialist, and so deep down we both knew this was something that could cause concern. But he was never one to worry about anything until he knew for definite that there was anything to actually worry about.

Naturally, I wanted to go along to see the specialist with him, but Gerald wouldn't hear of it. As far as he was concerned, it was just a niggle that needed sorting out. He was a very private person and never liked to make a fuss, but after his appointment he came back with the news that he needed to have surgery as soon as possible.

It was obvious that this was more than 'just a bit of tummy trouble' because the procedure was going to be performed on a bank holiday. He didn't tell me at the time that the specialist had discovered a growth on his colon that needed to be removed as a matter of urgency. He didn't make any kind of fuss about it – that just wasn't his way – and so I didn't make a fuss about it either. It was unspoken between us, but we both knew it must be something serious, otherwise he wouldn't have been called in so quickly. We did our best to carry on as normal, and off he went to have the 'little' op – though it turned out to be anything but, as it ended up with his having part of his colon removed.

Just like when I had been in a similar situation back in my twenties, the word 'cancer' was never mentioned. We all hoped that Gerald would recuperate quickly and life would get back to normal. It wasn't to be. Soon after his hospital visit, Gerald's weight began to drop dramatically. He lost his appetite and it was clear that something was still attacking his body.

Even though he was in a lot of pain, Gerald never made a big fuss about being ill; it just wasn't his way. Even when he discovered he had only a few years left to live – the specialist estimated it would be a maximum of five – it wasn't something that he felt he wanted to share with me, or anyone else for that matter. It wasn't that he was keeping things from me, or that he didn't think I could handle it after what I had been through with Lawrence, it just wasn't his way to talk about his health.

Gerald started having chemotherapy and regular checks on his cancer. Throughout all his treatment, he would go back and forth without making any kind of fuss. In fact, the only thing that annoyed him was if any of his treatment interfered with his golf or court days! I remember trying hard to find things for him to eat because he had no appetite at all. He would always ask for sea bass or a soufflé, and now, whenever I see either of those things on a menu, I always think of him …

He quietly continued working as normally as possible, and gradually started to make arrangements to ensure his staff would be employed after he had gone. Three of his employees had worked for him for a very long time so he decided to sell his jewellery manufacturing business so that nobody else would have to deal with the extra paperwork and stress in the event he was not well enough to carry on working. He also continued his work as a magistrate as it was something he felt so passionately about.

I decided that I should stop working at Amanda so that I could spend as much time as possible with Gerald. While I found it hard to do – the shop had, after all, represented so much about myself and my independence as a woman – I knew it was the right decision. It would mean that we could have as much quality time as possible to offset his chemo days.

With his illness at the forefront of our lives, I decided that the time had come for me to stop smoking once and for all. At this stage, I was smoking about 30 a day. I would always have a cigarette on the go. In fact, if the phone rang, I used to light another, so I would somehow have two going. I told Mandy that I was going to quit and she said that she would join me. I never pressed her to tell me how many she was smoking at that time, but I know it was enough of a concern for her to want to stop, too.

The therapist Allen Carr was getting a lot of publicity at the time for his seminars on how to stop smoking and, even though it was quite expensive, Mandy and I agreed it would be worth going along to one. We went to his home for a four-hour session, during which we were allowed to have our 'four last cigarettes'. At one point in the afternoon, he used a form of hypnosis, but I didn't feel like I had gone under; in fact, I didn't feel any difference at all. But, once the session was over, I didn't even think about lighting another cigarette. Three weeks later, I lost my passport in Spain and became very stressed about being able to get home. I found a packet of cigarettes in a drawer and lit one up … I heard Allen Carr's words in my head saying, 'Will you really feel better after that cigarette?' Enough was enough. I have not touched another cigarette since.

CHAPTER 29

Meanwhile, the one constant in my life was my fundraising work for the Alzheimer's Society and the Sam Beckman Day Centre, run by Jewish Care, which had been set up to offer stimulation activities for people with memory impairment or dementia. Illness or not, we were still having a great social life together and playing lots of golf.

It was when we were away on a golf weekend while I was Captain of the Society of Jewish Lady Golf Captains that Gerald announced he had booked for us to play at Pebble Beach in California the following year. He wanted to make the best of our time together and so this was a big treat for both of us. Pebble Beach is one of those resorts where you have to book about a year in advance and he told me that he had booked us a tee time of 8.30am on Friday, 10 January 1990. Little did I know that he had actually arranged for us to go first-class on a trip around the world first! It went unsaid, but we both knew that it was going to be our last holiday together and so we decided that we would treat it as a second honeymoon.

But before that, we had a very exciting event to look forward to. Mandy had been selected to represent Great Britain at golf in the 1989 Maccabiah Games, a sort of Jewish Olympics, held in Israel every four years. Some 4500 athletes took part in the 1989 games with 45 countries represented. It was a fantastic honour for Mandy and it was wonderful for me to be there to support her. The camaraderie between all the competitors was fantastic and the British ladies golf team won a bronze medal and were thrilled with the result. We were also thrilled because, just days before Mandy went off to the Games, we discovered she was two months' pregnant.

Not long after the Games, I helped to organise the 10th anniversary celebration of the Alzheimer's Society, at which John Major was our guest of honour. It was our most prestigious event to date, and Cora Phillips and I were delighted with how the society was moving forward.

In February 1990, my gorgeous granddaughter Katie was born. She was perfect in every way and was born with masses of black hair and the most beautiful eyelashes. Her birth really lifted everyone's spirits. What made it even more special was that Gerald became besotted with her and couldn't get enough of her. She was not his blood grandchild, but no one would have ever known. One of my happiest memories is when Gerald and I were out in Spain at the flat and Mandy brought little Katie over to spend time with us. Gerald had been particularly unwell after his latest batch of chemo and Katie's visit was a real tonic to us all.

Being a grandmother is like being in the best club in the world and I was always determined to be as useful as I could. I decided right from the start that Katie would be dressed 'a la Amanda', even though the shop wasn't around any more. I loved being a grandmother – and I have to also admit, I love the fact that, if they cry, you can give them back! Joking aside, nothing gives me more pleasure than knowing I am helping someone. No one has ever

wanted to be needed as much as me, and having a grandchild was
a new dimension for me, as well as a diversion for Gerald and his
awful chemo.

CHAPTER 30

Before I knew it, we were off on our fantastic round-the-world trip. The first stop on our itinerary was Bangkok where we stayed at the Mandarin Oriental. What a fabulous way to start the trip of a lifetime! One day, we saw the most gorgeous little baby girl in the swimming pool who could only have been about a year old. Gerald and I were so enchanted by her and we got talking to her parents – one was Scottish and the other English, and they were a lovely couple – but we thought nothing more of it as we were always meeting nice people on our travels …

After Bangkok, we flew to Hong Kong, where we stayed at the Regent Hotel and had the most amazing panoramic view over the city. We spent about five days there, sightseeing and shopping. Boy, how we shopped! We then flew on to Melbourne, where we met up with Gerald's brother Alan, and had a wonderful time there, travelling along the Great Ocean Road. It was extraordinary to be driving along miles and miles of stunning coast road, with rainforests virtually on the other side of the road.

From Victoria, we went to Hayman Island, which was just pure paradise, and who should be there but the little swimming baby and her parents! We joined up with them for dinner, and guess who ended up going parasailing with them the next day? I phoned Mandy the night before and told her that I was going to try parasailing. She was horrified and said I was far too old for that kind of behaviour!

Yes, I was older than the majority of people there, but we were having such a wonderful time and it was important to make the most of every minute I had left with my darling Gerald. It was such a special time and I remember it all so vividly – like the time we went out for a midnight dinner cruise to the Great Barrier Reef on a glass-bottomed boat, an experience I'll never forget.

After that, we flew on to Sydney where we had a wonderful time with our dear friends Lynne and Viv Shore, with whom we spent New Year's Eve, and then we went to Hawaii, where we watched the dolphins frolicking from our hotel window in Honolulu. Then it was time to go to Los Angeles, where we picked up our car and set off for Pebble Beach.

Gerald had bought some prescription sunglasses while we were in Hong Kong. I didn't really think anything of it at the time, but, on our way to Pebble Beach, all of a sudden, he almost drove us off the cliff! Gerald hadn't realised that he was wearing tinted glasses and, as it gradually got darker, his dark tinted glasses only made things even worse. He jammed his brakes on, there was a terrible screech and suddenly the bonnet of the car ended up poised over the cliff. For a moment I thought that was it for the pair of us. I was terrified, but it seemed it wasn't our time to go just yet. Gerald remained completely calm, possibly because he knew his wife would go into full-on panic mode given half a chance. We managed to squeeze out of the car by opening doors gently, and we moved away from the road and held each other very tightly.

It was getting very dark by this time, and we had to try to get help. Off we went, knowing that we were going to have to knock on complete strangers' doors and hope that they would take pity on us. Luckily, there was an English couple who had heard the screech of our brakes from their home nearby and they were an absolute godsend. They invited us into their home, gave us a drink and called the rescue services for us. It was only then that Gerald and I realised that he had been wearing tinted glasses the whole time. He felt terrible about the situation, but things could have been a lot worse.

We were soon on our way back to the car. With the rescue services' help, we got it back on the road and, exhausted, drove on to our hotel. Even after all that drama, we still managed to make our tee time of 8.30am the next day, though needless to say our golf wasn't up to much. It was ironic that the whole trip had been planned around this game of golf that was definitely below par for both of us …

Notwithstanding our near-death drama, it was an incredible holiday. I was the happiest I had ever been in my life. Yes, it was tinged with sadness, but Gerald would never let me talk about his illness or what was going to happen him. He was fighting fit for the whole trip and determined that life wasn't over for him.

After Los Angeles, we drove to San Francisco, where we stayed at the Fairmont Hotel. While we were there we went up to the top floor on the outside lift to the bar and drank a birthday toast to our dear friend Ernie Bernberg – one half of the beautiful couple. Next, we went on to visit Alcatraz, Fisherman's Wharf and all the sights. We then flew on to Washington DC, where we met up with a friend of Gerald's who he had grown up with and was like a sister to him. We went everywhere in limos – it was just like being a Hollywood star. Then, to cap it all, we flew home on Concorde. It truly was the most amazing trip of a lifetime. I am sure that when

Gerald planned this trip he wanted it to be a memory that stayed with me for ever – and it has!

Remember how I said that through my life I have blocked out the bad so that there is plenty of room for good memories? This was one of those times that I will never forget.

CHAPTER 31

Back home in January 1991, it wasn't long until the bubble burst after our wonderful holiday and life started to become difficult again for Gerald. He had to have more chemotherapy and we both had to face up to the fact that we didn't have long left together. It was a very sad and scary time for both of us.

We tried to make the best of things. Gerald was adamant that he was going to continue his court sessions and we still managed to visit our place in Spain. If anyone asked him how he was, he would always just say, 'Fine, fine, fine.' Physically, he was looking very ill and gaunt. He had lost a lot of weight, but he was determined to keep working as a magistrate.

In 1992, the Passover Appeal was made at Jewish Care to all of the London rabbis, with the aim that they would pass on the information to their congregants. I was asked to speak about Alzheimer's disease. My speech followed one by Lord Jonathan Sacks and Lord Michael Levy. It was incredibly daunting, but it was a real honour and a fantastic opportunity to help spread awareness about the disease.

My speech proved to be very successful as I was then asked if I would organise a very special Alzheimer's Society party. The timing of the event coincided with the 25th anniversary of the St John Smith Square Orchestra. The amazing percussionist Evelyn Glennie was due to perform at the gala evening, and so I came up with the idea to get the two events together. Princess Alexandra, who was a patron of the Society, attended and I have a lovely photograph of myself and the Princess taken that evening.

The concert was followed by dinner with Princess Alexandra as the guest of honour. Somehow – don't ask me how, I couldn't believe it myself! – I was able to get the Roux brothers to donate their time and they cooked the most magnificent meal for us at St James's Palace. The trouble was, there were no usable kitchens there, so all of the cooking was prepared and finished in catering vans! It was still delicious enough for royalty.

I was there with my darling Gerald and it was my responsibility to play host to the Princess. We sat with her during the concert and she was absolutely wonderful to Gerald. I remember at the end of the concert I asked her if she needed anything and she gracefully replied: 'I'm fine – look after your husband, he needs you more than I do'. She had been sitting next to him and could see that the evening had been quite challenging for him, even though, as usual, he had made no fuss.

The week after the event, Gerald had to go in to hospital as he was very weak. Mandy, meanwhile, was heavily pregnant with her second child, and on 23 June 1993 she was booked in to have a Caesarean at 6.30pm. Mandy being Mandy, she also wanted to support her daughter Katie, who had her sports day at nursery school that afternoon.

As she was always such a competitive person – and still is! – she thought the right thing to do was to run in the mother's egg and spoon race. It didn't seem to occur to her that maybe, being nine months' pregnant, she might not be at her fittest to run the race, and she was quite disappointed when she came in last but one! To make things worse, little Katie started crying her eyes out and having a tantrum. It wasn't that she was embarrassed about her sporty mum nearly coming last, but she thought Mandy was hurting her soon-to-be-born baby brother by running the race.

After the race, Mandy went into hospital and, happily, gorgeous Oliver Lawrence was delivered at just gone 7pm that night, weighing 7lb 13oz. I remember that evening so vividly, going from new life at one hospital to the other extreme at another. As I dashed from one to the other, I went through a whole maelstrom of emotions. It was an extraordinary day. I now had two wonderful grandchildren, but Gerald was on borrowed time.

Happily, Gerald was out of hospital in time to hold Oliver at his circumcision, which was very momentous for all of us. He and I spent as much time as we could with the children and this seemed to help us get through some very dark times.

About three months had passed and I was getting ready to drive Gerald to court to do his usual magistrate's duty. The nurse came to give him his shower – by this stage he was too weak to look after himself and he didn't want me to get involved with that side of things. He told me that he didn't feel well enough to go to court, and that if he went he felt he would not be able to do justice to the defendants, so he asked me to phone and let them know. This was the moment when I knew that it was only a matter of time. It was the first and only time that he ever missed a court session.

That evening, which was a Friday, we were due to go to supper at our friends' Monica and Dennis' house – the same Monica who had introduced me to Lawrence all those years ago. Gerald wouldn't hear of my cancelling, so Monica suggested that she brought the food to us. Gerald was adamant that we would go to them and made a supreme effort to enjoy the evening, but it was all too much for him. Back at home, after the most awful night, Gerald was taken into hospital by ambulance.

The hospital staff could see immediately that he was extremely sick and didn't have long to live. I suppose Gerald and I had been kidding ourselves that, if we acted as normal as possible, then life would go on. The truth was we couldn't bear to let fate take over. It was as if we were clutching at every opportunity to live life until the bitter end. That's why he continued to work for so long and why we always said yes to invitations. *Carpe diem* and all that.

The hospital staff were so kind. They gave me a spare room opposite Gerald's where my friends and family could come and support both of us. Mandy brought Oliver (who was all of three months at the time) every day and he certainly helped to lighten the mood. It was wonderful because it meant that Gerald had as much privacy as possible and that friends and family were there to support him and he was able to say his goodbyes properly. Six days after being taken into hospital, on 23 September 1993, my darling Gerald died, aged 69. I was with him for the whole time during his stay in hospital, and it was only when I went out of the room for a few minutes that he allowed himself to slip away. It was as if he was waiting for me to leave before he let go. He was such a private man, right up until the end.

Gerald had always insisted that he should be cremated – he said he wanted to 'kill the disease' once and for all. I found this hard to come to terms with; as a rule, Jewish people bury the dead rather than cremate. But, back when he was first diagnosed with terminal cancer, Gerald had arranged for us to meet with the wonderful Hugo Gryn, who was an esteemed rabbi and Holocaust survivor. Hugo understood Gerald's reasons for wanting to be cremated and managed to convince me that it was the right thing to do.

At the funeral, Gerald was praised for his tireless efforts on behalf of the British Jewellers' Association, his work as a Justice of the

Peace and his commitment to the Alzheimer's Society. His son Martin gave a beautiful eulogy and spoke eloquently about Gerald's loyalty and modest uncomplaining endurance: 'Our father spent his life making beautiful and enduring things, and in defending authenticity and in striving to do justice.'

There were over 500 people at his funeral and I received around the same number of wonderful condolence letters; I appreciate that people find it hard to know what to write on these occasions, but I found their kind words a huge comfort. Their support made me realise even more that I had been blessed with having two very special men in my life.

CHAPTER 32

There was no way I could ever have known that my time with Gerald would only amount to ten years, and that for five of those he would have a terminal illness. It all just seemed so unfair. Why was it that other people could meet someone, fall in love, have a family and live a long happy life, when I just seemed to have bad luck following me around?

When Lawrence had died, it had been very different. It's not that I didn't love him, of course, but it had been a kind of release as he had been so ill for such a long time. But Gerald had all his mental faculties right up until the end, and so the loss somehow felt more severe. I had lost a wonderful friend and it all felt incredibly raw. I began to wonder if I would ever be able to get close to someone again without bringing them horrendous luck.

Mandy was tremendously supportive during this time, but she had two children to take care of and her marriage was going through a tricky time. It had been in difficulties for a while and she had secretly been hoping that a new baby would patch up their marriage.

Meanwhile, while I was sitting shiva for Gerald, my flat was bursting at the seams with well-wishers. My friends Sonia, Pauline, Monica, Stella, Valerie and Lynne were there the whole time, preparing meals and making tea and coffee for everyone. But, once the mourning period was over, I was back on my own, and it hit me how alone I felt.

I tried to cope as best I could, and Sonia, Teri and Pauline all insisted that I go to Marbella and spend some time in the sunshine with them at their respective holiday homes. I had already started to mope around. My whole life had been focused around Gerald for the last few years and suddenly I had acres of free time to fill. I suppose I forgot how to live. I hoped some time away would hold the answer for how I could come to terms with my life again.

My first week in Spain was spent very quietly with Sonia and her husband Alf. It gave me a chance to reply to the condolence letters I had received. Sonia and Alf really looked after me, letting me have lots of time to talk about Gerald, to cry and to get frustrated about the unfairness of life. They were very kind. It is times like that that you really discover who your true friends are.

The second week was spent with other friends, Teri and Ernie, which was also great, but in a different way. Bill Large, who was a golf pro, and his lovely wife Joyce were also staying with them so it was a good distraction as they forced me to play as much golf as possible – which was always a great mood-lifter for me. It helped me focus on something other than mourning. After that, I went to stay with my dearest friend Pauline. Pauline was a bit like my mother, in that you either liked or disliked her and, like Mummy, she was a real character.

I was delighted to be with her, and I started thinking that maybe I should move to the same development as her and make a new start. I had also decided that I didn't want to go back to the flat Gerald had bought us. I couldn't face being there without him, surrounded by memories, so I sold up and was very fortunate to be able to buy a lovely apartment where Pauline was. Now, suddenly, I had a project to keep me busy, which was marvellous. I've always been able to cope so long as I'm kept busy.

The three weeks in Spain away from home did me a power of good. I shall always fondly remember my dear friends who made it happen; they really pulled me through a horrible time. Sadly, not one of those lovely friends is still alive today.

When I returned home to London, the British Jewellers' Association got in touch saying they wanted to organise a lunch at Goldsmiths' Hall as a tribute to Gerald. I was thrilled, but I felt it might be more fitting to have something that would memorialise him for years to come rather than just an expensive one-off event. And so the Kayman Award was established. The award is aimed at small businesses that combine craftsmanship and professionalism to create truly original work, and highlights the very best craft within the British jewellery industry. Working on the Kayman Award gave me an enormous amount of pleasure and allowed me to reflect on Gerald's talent and craftsmanship. It is still presented bi-annually at the spring fair in Birmingham and is a testament to how well respected Gerald was among the trade.

As the months went on, I tried to immerse myself in normal life and form new routines. I continued my work with the Alzheimer's Society and worked on my golf day committee. The fact that I have always kept myself involved has helped me get through whatever challenges I have had to face.

CHAPTER 33

In September 1993, I remember thinking that the following May I was going to reach another landmark birthday and turn 60. If Gerald had still been alive, I would have planned a special celebration, but without him I just wanted to go out with Mandy and the family. Gerald had promised that he would treat me to a facelift for my 60th birthday after I had nagged him for it, but it never happened. In hindsight, I feel better growing old gracefully – or even disgracefully!

Although I had no intention at that time of moving to Spain permanently, I decided to go ahead with furnishing my new flat at my friend Pauline's block, so that it would be really lovely for Mandy and the children when they came to visit. That way, perhaps, they would be tempted to stay for even longer.

The months flew by and my 60th birthday arrived. I was sad to be without Gerald, but I tried to look happy when Mandy and her husband came to pick me up to take me out to dinner. We were also going out with Lynne and Vivian, some other dear friends of mine. When we arrived there, they said they weren't quite ready so asked us in for a drink. In we went and, lo and behold, Lynne and Mandy had organised a surprise party with all of my dear friends … Sonia and Alf, Pauline, Stella and Johnnie, Valerie and Arthur and so many others, including my darling granddaughter Katie, were all there to celebrate. What an evening! I'll never forget how amazing the meal was and how much effort had gone into it. I felt incredibly special.

After I had blown out the candles, I really did have to face up to my life without Gerald. Mandy has always been a little sad that she never had brothers or sisters and I think she felt it even more when Gerald passed away, as it was almost as if she had lost two fathers. Within six months, she left her husband, who was 23 years older than her. In a similar way to other relationships she'd had, she had been looking for a father figure when she met him, but it just wasn't meant to be. At the time Katie was just three and little Oli was still a baby.

About this time, I started to have trouble with my speaking voice and I had to have intensive vocal therapy. The specialist attached electrodes, which were connected to a computer, to my vocal cords, and then helped me to pitch my speech patterns more effectively. I couldn't help thinking that, if the technology had been around 20 years earlier, maybe I would have been able to sing again. Nevertheless, I was incredibly grateful that I could speak again.

During this time, Mandy was finding life really tough. The banks were trying to foreclose on her home and it was a miracle that we found a firm who fought the banks on her behalf. She had to do all sorts of jobs to help support herself and the family. She had always been wonderful with children so one of her jobs was as a nursery school teacher in north London, and fortunately her daughter Katie was able to go to that school. She was very popular and loved by all.

I threw myself into being as good a grandmother as I could be and spent a lot of time with the children. When they were small, I took them to Disneyland Paris as a treat. This was the first time I had been there and we had a marvellous time. I remember walking in the gardens, reading about all the wonderful things we could do when – woopsy! – I fell down a hole. It made the rest of the time a little difficult, but we still had a great time.

I've always tried to give my grandchildren treats, but not spoil them, just as I had always insisted with my parents and Mandy. When Katie started school, I was there to pick her up in the afternoons, and I loved to take her out on trips whenever I could. Little Oli was growing very handsome and his lovely smile constantly reminded me of Lawrence. Catching glimpses of him was always such a comfort to me and meant that he was still alive in all of our hearts.

CHAPTER 34

In 1997, four years after Gerald had died, I decided to try to start a new life for myself in Spain. Mandy was busy working, bringing up the two children and rebuilding her social life. I was also spending more and more time in Marbella, as I had made some new friends there since Gerald died and had lots of friends from London who had second homes in the Marbella area. I was also a member of a rather nice golf club there – and let's not forget the weather is generally better, so it ticked all the boxes.

I found that as a single woman I was better accepted over there as there seemed to be more people in the same boat. I was always being invited to dinner parties and bridge afternoons, and gradually I started to have people over myself. I hadn't really thrown parties on my own before, so it was a bit daunting at first. But everyone that I mixed with in Marbella seemed so friendly and welcoming.

In London, I really felt that, as a widow, people were reticent to invite me over. I know it is an old-fashioned idea, but, in that generation, friends very much went out as couples – unless, that is, there was some (usually quite unsubtle) matchmaking going on. I would arrive somewhere and discover that so and so's single friend was invited along to make up the numbers. But, as I had made it clear from the outset that I didn't have any interest in meeting anyone at that time, back at home the invitations weren't really forthcoming.

After going back and forth to Marbella on several occasions, I decided to sell the flat I had lived in with Gerald in Highgate in north London and moved over to Spain permanently. I wanted to make a new start, even though I knew it would mean I was out of the London property market. To people who live outside London, this may not seem like a big deal, but, with property values rising all the time, you have to be in the market to make the most of its appreciation.

I decided that I would spend around six weeks at a time in Spain, and then go home to London to catch up with friends and the family. I was able to stay with Mandy, so I could spend as much time as I wanted with my grandchildren. They would also have a lovely place where they could come over for long weekends and any other time they fancied a break.

I could also continue to be involved with the Alzheimer's Society while I was over there and, as I still intended to come back to London regularly, I could still work on fundraising events.

I really wanted to get on with my life in the best way I could. I tried not to feel too sorry for myself; I am a firm believer that things happen for a reason – *que sera, sera* had very quickly become my catchphrase in life. I knew that something positive had come out of Lawrence's illness as it was a springboard to getting the Alzheimer's Society started. And having watched Gerald's incredible strength of character in the last months of his life gave me the determination to continue with the work that I felt so passionately about.

I remember a friend of mine being absolutely incredulous about my bad luck, saying I must have done something very bad in a past life to have had so many terrible things thrown at me. But even though I could have wallowed in some very low points in my life, it is just not in my nature. Yes, I might be a bit fed up for a day or so, but I've always been able to see a different side to a situation. After all, it wasn't me who had to go through the pain of cancer or the personal devastation of Alzheimer's.

And, once again, there was romance on the horizon.

One night in Spain, I went to my friend Victor's 'second bar mitzvah' celebration, which was his way of celebrating his 83rd birthday. At the party, I met a very nice man called David, who was living in nearby Calahonda. He had lost his wife a few years earlier, so the two of us had quite a lot in common. He was a super dancer and we had a lovely evening together. I was leaving for London the next day, but I promised him I would call him on my return.

It was still only four years since I had lost Gerald so I never saw it as anything serious. But I thought it would be nice to keep in touch with him as we had got on so well and it was nice to have a new male friend. So, as promised, I called him on my return to Spain. We picked up where we had left off and, although neither of us had planned any kind of romance, we quickly fell into an easy relationship together. Almost without realising it, we became an item.

Within a few months – and I have to say at this point that this wasn't my idea and I said I thought it was too quick and that we should wait – he sold his flat and moved in with me. Encouraged by friends who urged us to get together, we were swept along by the idea of being a couple. We were two eligible single people who had lots in common and lots of life to live.

Although we got on very well and enjoyed each other's company, this kind of relationship wasn't what I wanted. I knew it was too soon for me. I suppose I had hoped that I would be as happy in a couple with David as I had been with Gerald, sharing meals and the minutiae of life, being happy to just be. If anything, though, I felt even more lonely because I knew the feeling just wasn't there for either of us, and it wasn't too long before we went our separate ways.

CHAPTER 35

I remember celebrating the Millennium at the home of my friends Gloria and Victor Benjamin in Spain – the same Victor who had celebrated his second bar mitzvah where I had met David. It was fantastic and their home was a wonderful venue for such a milestone. I had known Victor for most of my life, as my parents had been friendly with him and his first wife Jean through the Goodkinds. All the crowd were invited, so it was almost like being with family. As usual, Mandy and I spoke to each other at 11 o'clock and then again at 12 o'clock, covering the midnight hour in both countries.

Like almost everyone, it seemed, I felt that I had a newfound optimism for the new century, and so I decided to treat myself and go on a cruise. I was quite happy with my own company so I wasn't fazed at all by the idea that I would be stepping on board alone. I booked the *Radisson Navigator*, flew to Miami and joined the ship to cruise through the Panama Canal. Before I went, Mandy and lots of my girlfriends were teasing me about having a holiday romance! Even though I said that was definitely not the idea of the trip at all, they gave me strict instructions to make sure that I went to the Friday night Jewish service – just in case there was a likeminded gentleman there – and to the singles' evening. I promised them I would, even though I kept stressing that I was quite happy on my own.

It was just my luck that the singles' night was on a Friday, so I decided to miss the Friday night service and make an effort for the singles' night instead. Oh well, in for a penny, in for a pound, as they say ... I booked a hair appointment, but they took so much time that I only just made it for the last 20 minutes of the cocktail party. Luck was on my side, though, as, just as I walked into the party, a very nice-looking man was also arriving at the same time. We hit it off straight away as we struck up a very silly flirty conversation and had a lovely evening together. What's more, our newfound friendship continued for the rest of the cruise! I later discovered that I was lucky to meet him, because he was the only single man there and there were many single ladies. It must have been the new hairdo!

His name was Michael and he lived in New York. His late wife had suffered from Motor Neurone Disease, so there was an immediate empathy between us as we shared a lot of common ground. Although Michael was over 10 years older than me, that didn't bother me and our friendship went on to be more than just a holiday fling. Once I was back in Spain, he started calling me straight away and the phone calls continued, together with deliveries of flowers and cards. It wasn't too long before I was waiting at Malaga airport for him when he came to visit. I had booked him into the newly opened Kempinski hotel, which was near my apartment, but he soon left the hotel and joined me.

From that time on for the next two years, I was either flying to New York to stay with him or he was flying to Marbella or London to be with me. It was a lovely time. Friends were thrilled that I was enjoying a glamorous new romance.

When I was in New York, he took me to the Metropolitan Opera House, and I remember seeing *La bohème* with him, after we had dinner in the Metropolitan restaurant. He had a permanently reserved table there as he was a patron of the opera house. He treated me wonderfully and I have to say I loved every minute.

One year, he asked me to join him for the summer in Lake Saranac in upstate New York as he had a country home there. I was invited to stay for six weeks, which seemed a very long time to be away from home in Spain and so far away from Mandy and the grandchildren. But he had made it sound so magnificent that I couldn't resist. I could imagine the tennis courts leading down magnificent lawns to the boathouse and the lake. It sounded like the Great Gatsby!

But nothing is ever quite what you imagine. Yes, the house was lovely, but it lacked a woman's touch – not that I wanted to provide it! – and it all felt very cold to me, despite the fact that it was baking hot outside. The lake was indeed at the bottom of the garden, so was the boathouse, but the house was screened by enormously tall trees, which made me feel really claustrophobic and I felt uncomfortable right from the start. I began to feel suffocated, not only by the trees, but by Michael, too. I felt that he wanted to own me like one of his possessions and I suddenly panicked. It all just felt wrong. Although I had originally intended to stay for the whole of the summer, I knew that it wasn't right for me and I decided to leave after a fortnight. The sparkle had somehow faded between us and I flew back to New York and picked up a flight to London.

We both knew it was over, but there were no regrets. It was just one of those things, and so it all ended quite amicably between us. It had been a very good couple of years together and we had both enjoyed the relationship, but deep down we both knew that it wasn't 100 per cent right. We could have carried on as we were, but it would have been just going through the motions rather than really feeling we should be together. When you have really truly been in love, nothing comes close to that feeling, and you end up acting out a role that you are not totally comfortable playing.

On the flight back from Michael's house in New York, it suddenly struck me that I should be returning to London for good. After feeling so uncomfortable at his house, I felt a real hankering to be home with my family, rather than it just being a visit en route to Marbella. I realised my heart was very much in Britain, even though all of my material possessions were in Spain.

As soon as I saw Mandy and the kids at the airport, I cried and cried, and within days I was convinced that selling up in Spain and coming back to live in London would be the right thing for me to do. It would take time to pack up my life over there, of course, but as adamant as I had been about moving over there in the first place, I was sure I should come home now. What made it even more lovely was the fact that Mandy and the children were thrilled – even if it meant they couldn't have so many free holidays in Spain!

I went back to Spain a few days later with plans to move by the end of the year. I settled back into my usual routine and planned to enjoy catching up with friends before thinking about selling.

CHAPTER 36

Shortly after I went back to Spain, one lunchtime I got a very alarming call from Mandy. It was 11 September 2001 and she told me to switch on the television. While she watched in London and I watched in Spain, we saw the horrific terrorist attacks on the Twin Towers of the World Trade Center in New York. It was so awful to watch and I remember thinking, 'What the hell am I doing in Spain when my nearest and dearest are in London? Get on with that move, Morella!'

What finally made up my mind for me was much less dramatic, but it seemed quite frightening at the time. During a very ordinary trip to the supermarket on one of my visits back to London, I reached for a pint of milk and the next thing I knew a woman was standing over me saying I had collapsed. I was immediately rushed to hospital, and when I was feeling less muddle-headed I was told that in all likelihood my funny turn had been an epileptic seizure.

I had never suffered anything like that before. I couldn't understand it as I hadn't done anything differently. My diet was the same, I was getting lots of sleep and I hadn't been dehydrated or anything like that. It was a total mystery, but there was nothing I could do about it. I was immediately put on epilepsy medication and I was terribly upset about the prospect of living with the condition. The fact that I wouldn't be able to drive and that I might not be able to live as independently as before horrified me. I was told that I just had to take things easier, and that was that.

A month or so later, when I felt a bit better, I went to Spain for some sunshine, but I'd made up my mind that I wouldn't be staying there. I duly put the flat on the market and arranged for my things to be shipped back to Mandy's.

For a year after the 'epilepsy' incident in the supermarket, I didn't have even the suggestion of another funny turn, so after a long discussion with my GP I stopped taking the medication and life went back to normal. I've never had any kind of attacks since. I can't help thinking that maybe I was mis-diagnosed at the time. The annoying thing was I couldn't drive until the year was over, but apart from that it was just one of life's blips. *Que sera, sera.*

After living with Mandy for a while, I thought it was high time that I got back on my own two feet and I bought a nice flat in a block in Edgware in north London. As I always like to make new friends wherever I am, I soon became friends with my neighbour Alan. He was unattached and we became great companions. It was lovely to go to the theatre and the cinema with him and we enjoyed a great friendship for the next few years.

In fact, we got on so well that, when we heard about a new development being built in Stanmore, we decided to buy flats next door to each other. This was 2003 and I hoped that this would be my last move for some time. Since my marriage to Lawrence, I had moved six times in London, then I moved to Spain and lived in four different places, and I'd had another three moves since my return to London! Enough was enough!

The apartment block that we liked was at the end of a building project that was being built on an old RAF base. The flat I particularly liked overlooked a park and the only noise I could hear were the ducks and swans in the pond that ran alongside the flats. It was such an idyllic setting, and Alan and I were thrilled when we each got our keys.

We continued to be wonderful companions together and went on some really lovely holidays, including one to Las Vegas and another cruising to Hawaii. We were in Boston at the time of the 2004 American election, and it was very exciting as our hotel was being used as the campaign HQ. We really felt like we were part of the action.

Back at home in London, Alan and I would often eat out together or I'd cook something and we watched TV. Alan was quite an avid reader so, if he didn't like some of the TV that I liked to watch, he read. We were great friends, but nothing more.

If only I had been prepared to settle for this life that was comfortable, without too much excitement, that could have been the start of a lovely calm chapter of my life. Alan was a lovely, trustworthy, kind and reliable friend. But, looking back, I suppose it's never been in my nature to just have a quiet life and not crave the next adventure. I've always been a person who looks for excitement at every turn.

When I was 70, Mandy threw a ladies' lunch for me at the very smart Grove Hotel in Watford. There were probably about 20 women there, all of whom had been my friends for many years. We ate, we drank, we made speeches, and we had a lot of fun. That same evening, I had arranged a car to take Mandy, Katie, Oli and a friend of Mandy's to Gatwick, from where we were going to fly to Orlando. On the way in the car, the driver put on a CD and the next moment I heard my granddaughter Katie singing with my grandson Oli playing the saxophone. It was such a lovely present and off we flew to Orlando for two weeks. I don't remember ever having so much fun – even when I went on a ride that no 70-year-old should go on!

We have always made a big thing about birthdays and it is my belief that you should always try to find things to celebrate. My daughter agrees and that holiday she took things even further. Whatever restaurant we went into during our stay, she told the staff that it was my birthday. After two weeks and at least fourteen birthday cakes, it was little wonder that I put on a bit of weight!

CHAPTER 37

In 2004, a friend of mine who worked at Jewish Care told me that, because of my fundraising and awareness work for dementia, Jewish Care wanted to dedicate a plaque at the Sam Beckman Centre in memory of Lawrence. This came totally out of the blue and I was incredibly moved by the gesture. To mark the unveiling of the plaque, my family, the committee and close friends were invited along to the dedication, where we had tea with many of the users of the centre. It was wonderful to see the facilities in action. Naturally, I was tearful with the memory of Lawrence, but it was a wonderfully comforting afternoon and it was lovely to be surrounded by friends.

The following summer, I received a letter from the Head of Campaigns at the CSV (Community Service Volunteers). The letter was to inform me that I had been nominated for an inspiration award at the Year of the Volunteer Awards. They said they were delighted to announce that I had got through the first round of judging, that there would be a shortlist of potential winners per category and these would be notified before 31 August 2005. I was thrilled to bits as it was totally unexpected, but it was really lovely to even have been considered for something like this. When you do any kind of charity work, you don't start thinking about what you are going to get in return – that's not the spirit of it at all. Nevertheless, it is always nice to be appreciated.

A couple of weeks later, I heard that I had been selected as one of the fifty medal recipients from London who would go through to the next round as champions in the regional categories. It was all very exciting and humbling to be among the list of some very inspirational people. Soon after, I got an invitation to a reception at Drury Lane on Sunday, 22 January 2006. This would be before the award ceremony at which the category champions were announced.

I was one of 2,005 nominees who had made it to the final 45-strong shortlist for the event, and I was really proud of myself. I was never the cleverest at school and certainly didn't win any academic awards, so it was lovely to be considered for something like this. I went along with Mandy, and the first person to greet us when we got to the reception was the President of the CSV, Lord Levy, who was most welcoming and complimentary. He is also President of Jewish Care, so I had met him previously.

It was a very exciting afternoon and, while we had drinks, new friendships were made before the formalities began. The TV presenter Jon Snow was the host of the afternoon and, although I wasn't the outright winner for my category, I received a commemorative medal, which had been struck by the Royal Mint. It was a wonderful afternoon and all of us volunteers felt very special for having been invited there.

In March 2007, I attended another special lunch. This one was to mark the beginning of an important new phase in the work of the Alzheimer's Society. It was hosted by Lord Morris of Manchester and I was thrilled to attend. I sat between two actors,

Lynda Bellingham and Kevin Whately. The whole day was immensely interesting as we got to hear about new research into dementia and the scientific studies that were making a significant impact on the treatment of the condition.

It was events like these – the unveiling of the plaque for Lawrence, being involved in the volunteers' awards and the ongoing research into dementia – that really seemed to make sense of my life. Unfortunately, there are chapters of my life that I totally regret – and the following is definitely one of those!

CHAPTER 38

I had been extraordinarily lucky to have had not one, but two wonderful husbands already, not to mention a number of romances with other men. Yet, no matter what I do, I just can't help my flirtatious nature. I am in love with the idea of being in love. I always have been and I think I always will.

At this time, Mandy had met with an unofficial matchmaker called Clare. She wasn't a dating agent or anything like that, she just got a kick out of playing Cupid. I don't think that's particularly unusual – I'm always thinking of who would be lovely with so and so when I discover they are single.

Mandy had mentioned me to Clare and vice versa, and so eventually I went along to meet her. She told me about a man she knew whom she thought I might like to meet. She remembered him from her own single days, but didn't know too much about him other than what he told her. She said that, like me, he was very confident and chatty, and that we would get along like a house on fire. She also said he was very good-looking!

'Sammy' phoned me and straight away I liked his voice and thought, oh yes, this could be interesting … The only trouble was, I had just had laser treatment on my eyes and I wasn't exactly looking my best, so I said I couldn't meet him until I could wear make-up again. We arranged to meet for coffee at a smart hotel in Watford. I thought we might as well start how we meant to go on and kick off our friendship somewhere lovely.

I was quite excited about meeting him and got to the hotel early so I could position myself to see him easily as he walked in. I actually pretended to be on the phone so that I could get the measure of him as he walked towards me. I have to say I was instantly attracted to him. He was tall, very attractive and we immediately got on like a house on fire. We talked and talked and talked, and even discovered that we had a distant cousin in common. He was a great conversationalist; he made me laugh and was really charming. He complimented me, telling me he couldn't believe that he would meet anyone as vivacious and attractive as me, and I was totally smitten. Our meeting for coffee went on for three hours, and so we stayed and had lunch, too, as the conversation just flowed.

As well as finding out that he too was distantly related to the Goodkind family, I discovered that he had grown up in north-west London. But he didn't dwell too much on his past. He just said that he had been married twice before, that he was recently widowed and spoke about his late wife very fondly. I was touched by how sincere he was, as they had obviously had a very deep and meaningful relationship. Sammy told me he had fallen out with his children but didn't say much more about that. As it was our first meeting, I didn't want to press him for any details. I certainly wasn't about to spoil things and start interrogating him with twenty questions. Quite honestly, I felt like I'd died and gone to heaven.

I never thought that at my age I would be likely to have the same kind of feelings I'd had as a teenager, but the chemistry was quite electric! I think I knew right from the start that this would become more than just a platonic relationship, and I couldn't wait to tell Mandy and my close friends about this wonderful man I had met. When I got home later that afternoon, I was straight on the phone to Mandy, telling her every little detail and she was delighted for me.

Within weeks, I had totally fallen for him and invited him to join me in Spain, which he duly did. We had a fabulous time together. I knew he had been married twice before, but so had I, so obviously it didn't bother me. I told him that what was past had passed and that I was only interested in the future. As far as I could see it, we were totally made for each other. It was fate that we had both been widowed and that we had found each other later in life. We had gone through a turbulent past, but could settle into a fabulous future together. Lady Luck was smiling down on us.

Shortly after returning home from Spain, Sammy moved into my flat and we officially became an item. I never stopped to think why it was that he was estranged from his son and, although I thought at the time it was unusual that a successful businessman in his mid-seventies didn't have a proper income, I put it to the back of my mind. We were very much in love and it didn't seem to matter.

Those first few months were bliss. We got on fabulously. Mandy really seemed to like him and she and my friends were delighted to see me so happy again with my new boyfriend. However, after a few months, Mandy had a strange phone call from a family member, who told her to try to discourage my relationship with Sammy because he had a reputation as a bit of a womaniser.

Mandy was upset and told me straight away, hoping that it wouldn't be true, but knowing I had to be told. I was so blinded by my infatuation that I said I believed that whatever had happened in the past was in the past. I was madly in love with him. I told her I felt truly happy for the first time since being with Gerald.

I heard various rumours during the next few months, but Sammy reassured me that there was nothing to worry about. In March 2008, he asked me to marry him. I kept saying that I didn't think it was necessary in this day and age, that we could carry on the way we were quite happily, but he tried to convince me that it was the right thing to do and that he was looking forward to the rest of our lives together.

He kept on proposing until eventually, on Mother's Day 2009, he 'got through to me', as he put it. I suppose I was caught up in the moment; we were drinking champagne at the time and it was lovely and romantic. I thought, Why not? I knew that not all of my friends were as crazy about him as I was, but I'd always believed you have one life and you should grab it with both hands.

We decided that we would get married at my golf club, and started making all the arrangements. We wanted a party that everyone invited could enjoy and let their hair down at, so we invited around a hundred friends and my family. The wedding was on 7 July 2009 and the weather could not have been worse, which, of course, I should have seen as an omen …

We had hoped that the sun would be shining and that we would be able to have the ceremony outside. But the heavens opened and it was rain, hail, thunder and lightning all the way to Dyrham Park. While in the car, I began to worry that maybe someone up there was not happy about what I was about to do, but I dismissed these thoughts as quickly as they came. Mandy gave me away and Katie sang for us. It was just fabulous.

The whole thing was great fun. We had an Abba tribute group who were fantastic and all our guests spent the evening dancing and singing along. The dinner lived up to what was expected of Dyrham Park and everyone let their hair down as we had hoped. The following day, together with our friends Sonia and Alf, we travelled by car to Honfleur in France for a 'mini-moon'. I know it's not exactly traditional to bring your best friends on your honeymoon, but the four of us got on really well. After all, I was used to sharing my honeymoon, as my parents had turned up when I was on honeymoon with Lawrence. It almost felt traditional!

As soon as the honeymoon was over, cracks in our relationship started to show. It was silly things to start with, such as Sammy complaining that I kept interrupting him and that it was extremely rude. Then I felt he was giving me the silent treatment and I never knew why. I suggested that we went to a couple's counsellor. He was reluctant at first, but eventually agreed.

To cut a very long story short, we eventually split up in February 2010 after a very traumatic few months. It took me a long time to realise the truth in the saying 'there's no fool like an old fool'. When something seems too good to be true, it usually is.

Before Sammy, I had thought my love life was over. It was hard to believe that at my age I could still meet a man and believe that I had died and gone to heaven. But, looking back, those years were anything but.

Because I was used to a certain amount of heartache in my life – first with Lawrence and then Gerald – I suppose I had become preconditioned to coping with difficult situations. I think that's why it took me longer than it should have done to admit that my relationship with Sammy wasn't right for me. It took me a long time to get my confidence back after the events of 2007–2010. As always, my wonderful family and friends supported me emotionally and helped me through the difficult times. I am incredibly lucky to have such a strong and devoted group of people around me who have been a tower of strength to me during such challenging times.

CHAPTER 39

As with the other traumatic times in my life, I tried to pick myself up, dust myself off and start thinking of the next project. I decided that, as my work for the Alzheimer's Society and Jewish Care has always been a mainstay of my life, I should try to throw myself into helping further in this direction, possibly for the first time actually trying to help and support those suffering from the disease itself. And, if my personal life was to become difficult again, I could take solace in working to this end.

Coincidently, around this time, a close friend of mine who had been diagnosed with Alzheimer's disease a few years previously was at a stage where I thought it would be helpful for her to enjoy activities provided by a day centre, such as discussion groups, playing cards or getting involved in some kind of music group.

My golf day had always supported the Sam Beckman Day Centre in Hendon, so it seemed the obvious place for her to spend a day or so each week. I took her and her husband to see the centre, and it was decided that she would go along for a few weeks to see if she liked it there. I picked them up and she seemed to settle down quite well. Even if she wasn't able to participate in all the activities, she always seemed to enjoy herself to the best of her ability. The day at the centre was good for her and it was also good for her husband, who was able to do things on that day that he couldn't do when his wife was at home with him – silly things like changing light bulbs and getting up to date with paperwork.

Around that time, I was invited to go along to a relatively new initiative in London called Singing for the Brain, which the Society had developed as a music therapy for people with dementia and Alzheimer's. It had been trialling in various areas in the UK, and more and more centres were gradually opening up. Singing for the Brain is a group activity that uses singing to help stimulate the memory and provides a way for people with dementia to socialise together. It also gives carers an opportunity to meet, share experiences and support each other.

On the occasion I was invited along, the session was at the Liberal Jewish Synagogue in the borough of Westminster. I really didn't know what to expect and assumed it would be a lovely singalong session, but nothing more really.

Well, I watched, I listened, I laughed, I cried. I was gobsmacked! The sheer energy of the session facilitator was an absolute joy to experience and the songs and vocal exercises that she did with the group had the most incredible effect on everybody there. It all starts with a cup of tea or coffee so that the 'clients' and carers can get together and catch up. It is also a lovely way to meet new likeminded friends, and carers can discuss how they cope with tricky situations and other worries they might have. After that, the facilitator gets everyone into a circle with a special song: 'Welcome one and all, welcome one and all, come and join the circle, welcome one and all …' This is repeated until everyone is seated and ready to sing. The idea is that over time the clients become familiar with the melody and know it's a signal for the singing to start.

The great thing is that you don't need to be musical at all and you can join in as much or as little as you feel like. First the facilitator goes around the circle singing the hello song, so she'll sing 'He-llo Morella', which everyone repeats, then she goes on to the next person and so on. This is followed by warm-up exercises, very often to a jolly song so everyone can tap their feet, shake arms in the air and generally loosen up, then a lovely relaxing breathing session to get everyone ready to sing. Simple songs are sung, tapping out the rhythm on beanbags, together with easy-to-follow action songs, rhythm games and percussion exercises that everyone is encouraged to join in with. If mistakes are made, it's no problem at all, it all just adds to the fun.

I would never have believed that something as simple as this could have such a profound effect on someone with Alzheimer's disease. Watching clients arrive with seemingly no life behind their eyes and then seeing their memory sparked as a piece of music is played is a wonderful thing. To see a smile developing as it triggers a long-forgotten memory, a completely impulsive need to tap the feet and sometimes even the urge to get up to dance is quite extraordinary.

I was so enraptured by the whole experience that the following week I took my friend and her husband along to a session. It was heartwarming to watch the joy on his face while watching his wife enjoy herself – he hadn't seen such animation from her in years. I could see him falling in love with her all over again.

I couldn't help thinking how lovely it would have been for me and Lawrence if something like Singing for the Brain had been around at the time he was ill. I know that it wouldn't have changed the end result, but to have been able to share something as simple as doing actions to 'The Grand Old Duke of York' would have been a refreshing distraction from the frustration of his locked-in life. Although some of the songs may sound a little childlike, they stimulate all kinds of emotions and take the group member, be it the client or carer, out of themselves. It's like flicking a switch and gradually seeing true personalities coming back to life.

The first Singing for the Brain session that I attended in Westminster had a profound effect on me and I knew it was something I wanted to get thoroughly involved in. Having trained to be a singer all those years ago, and having had my voice taken away from me, I saw this as a chance to bring music back into my life, which in turn made me start thinking of ways in which I could help with the funding for more sessions like these.

It would take a year or so until I could become fully involved with sessions of my own, as a series of events took place that became a springboard into the next period of my life.

CHAPTER 40

In May 2009, I was invited to the House of Lords, along with my family and committee members from the Alzheimer's Disease Golf Society, to an event hosted by Lord Julian Fellowes, who is best known as the writer of *Downton Abbey* but is also an ambassador for the Alzheimer's Society. The occasion was to launch a new Alzheimer's drug discovery programme, and a wonderful man called Peter Dunlop, who had been diagnosed with Alzheimer's in 2009, gave a speech about his experiences. He spoke from the heart about living with dementia and the importance of getting an early diagnosis in order to start taking medication, and he movingly explained how it had allowed him the time to have a better perspective about the future while being able to function more normally. Other speakers on the day included the recently appointed Chief Executive Jeremy Hughes and the Society's Director of Research, Professor Clive Ballard.

Fiona Phillips, the well-known television presenter who is also an ambassador for the Society, was also there and was signing copies of her book *Before I Forget*. It was a real pleasure and honour to meet her and hear her describe experiences of coping with both her parents living with Alzheimer's.

Things always seem to happen for a reason. Soon after my visit to Westminster, I received a phone call from Nick Doffman, the Chairman of the Topland Group Business Luncheon. He told me my name had been put forward by Jewish Care for an unsung hero award, in recognition of my 'ongoing commitment to raise money for those living with dementia'. I was gob-smacked and very excited. I was told that I would have to make a speech, which didn't especially worry me, until I heard that I would be speaking after the BBC's Business Editor Robert Peston. I was incredibly nervous, but I was so honoured to be involved.

Despite my nerves, my speech went down well. I focused on Singing for the Brain, explaining to the audience how beneficial it is to both client and carer, and how I would have loved my dearest Lawrence to have experienced it. It clearly had the desired effect as the event went on to raise in excess of £300,000, which was used to fund the deficit for Jewish Care's day-care centre for dementia.

After my speech, a very generous benefactor came over to me and asked me to phone him the next day, which I duly did. He invited me to a meeting with John Raffles from the Alzheimer's Society and he told us that he and his wife wanted to sponsor a new Singing for the Brain group for a minimum of three years. I was so happy. It meant that I could put plans in place for a brand-new Singing for the Brain venture, which would be the first joint partnership between the Society and Jewish Care. I was desperate for this amalgamation to take place as I had previously approached Simon Morris, the chief executive of Jewish Care, who was very supportive of my idea to get the two organisations working together as much as possible regarding dementia.

I felt very proud that a simple thing like a speech could trigger such generosity, which would end up having a profound effect on people's lives.

CHAPTER 41

One day in November 2011, I picked up my post and was shocked to find an envelope addressed to me from the Ceremonial Officer at the Cabinet Office. It read:

> The Prime Minister has asked me to inform you, in strict confidence that, having accepted the advice of the cabinet secretary and the main honours committee, he proposes to submit your name to the Queen recommending that Her Majesty may be graciously pleased to approve that you be appointed a Member of the Order of the British Empire (MBE) in the New Year 2012 Honours List.

Wow! How do you react to a letter like that? I kept thinking about how it was possible that an ordinary person like me could be nominated for an honour like this and wondered how it had come about. I assumed the Alzheimer's Society or Jewish Care had been involved with it somehow. You are not supposed to know, but some time later I saw copies of certain letters and realised that my guesses were probably right. Reading them, I found it hard to believe that they were written about me. Anyone who had gone through similar circumstances would have done the same thing as me.

I was very excited about the idea of receiving the honour, but it was also a bittersweet experience. I felt proud about what I had achieved, but none of it would ever have happened if I hadn't been married to a man who suffered so much at such a young age. At least I could take some comfort in the fact that the Alzheimer's Society is now helping many thousands of people in the same situation.

At that moment, though, what was really troubling me was how on earth I was going to keep this a secret from my family and friends. I have never kept anything secret from Mandy and, even though I wasn't meant to say anything to anyone about it, I called her straight away. Her reaction was priceless. 'Oh, thank God you know!' she laughed. 'I'm so sick of having to keep my mouth shut about it!'

In order to avoid spilling the beans to anyone else, I decided that I would put all my efforts into arranging a New Year's Eve party at which I would be able to share the news about my MBE with all my close friends and family. I found I actually ended up avoiding seeing people prior to New Year's Eve in case I let it slip. Something like that is extremely hard to keep secret for a chatterbox like me.

Somehow I managed to keep schtum until the party, and it was a great occasion. All the friends and family who had provided me with such great support over the years were there, though sadly not my dear friends Sonia and Alf. Sonia told me she was really tired and said she would try to come the following day to another lunch I had arranged at the golf club.

New Year's Eve was a great success and I was bubbling over with excitement about my news, which I shared with everyone, and I drank in the cheers and applause. It really was a wonderful night. I felt very proud of myself and so happy that my lovely Mandy could be so proud of me, too. After all that we had been through together, it was a lovely thing to be able to share.

The celebrations continued the following day at the lunch I had organised. Mandy, her partner Trevor, Katie and Oli were all there, but unfortunately Sonia still wasn't feeling up to it. Little did I know at that time that she was about to become very ill indeed. She was so thrilled about my honour, though, and I truly believe that in some way she made it her mission to be as involved as she could be in all the excitement to help her cope with the bad time that she was going through.

CHAPTER 42

Shortly after the New Year Honours list was announced, I went on holiday to South Africa with my dear friend Helen Davis. We had known each other for many years, due in some part to the generosity of her wonderful late husband Alfred. He had always supported the Alzheimer's Society and the various events that I had organised over the years. Helen and I had become close over the past few years and so the two of us decided to go on holiday together. Like me, she is always full of beans and loves travelling and socialising, so we knew we would be great holiday buddies.

We flew to Cape Town and stayed there for four nights before going on to the gourmet capital of South Africa, Franschhoek, for another four nights. My waistline measurement was testament to the fact it was a gourmet town. Oh, the meals we enjoyed! We then flew to George and drove 50 miles along the Garden Route to Plettenberg Bay. It was so beautiful and peaceful there, and we were very sad to leave when the time came. I'm ashamed to say it, but we ate and drank ourselves silly throughout the whole trip; I think

I celebrated the news of my MBE rather too much, but I was on such a high. Helen was quite happy to share the excitement, too – and the calories!

I knew that, once the holiday was over, I would have to start yet another diet. Like almost every other woman I have ever known, dieting is a fact of life for me. I've tried them all – fried breakfasts on the Atkins diets, Weight Watchers, Slimming World, Dukan, The F Plan, you name it, I've done it – but they only ever seem to work the first time I try them. I have done detox programmes, had colonic irrigation, counted calories, carefully weighed, juiced, fasted and generally given myself a hard time about food. But I've also had lots of beautiful rich meals and holidays where I throw caution to the wind – and the diet book out of the window – and that holiday to Cape Town was delicious from the word go.

As I know only too well, though, life is always full of ups and downs – and I was soon to come back down to earth with a very big bang when the holiday was over. On arriving home, the first thing I did, as always, was call Mandy. The moment I heard her voice, I could tell that something terrible had happened. It transpired that Sonia, my friend who couldn't make it to my parties over New Year, was in hospital. She had been diagnosed with cancer and the prognosis was not good. I couldn't get to the hospital quickly enough to see her.

When I saw her and her adoring husband Alf, I knew that I had to try to be upbeat, so when Alf left us alone together I told her all about the holiday and showed her all my photographs. Clicking into happy mode, she too did her best to be upbeat. To an outsider, it would appear as if we were just two friends catching up on all the news without a care in the world. For two hours, we distracted ourselves as I relived the holiday – and all of those meals – and she filled me in on news about her family. There was also lots of talk about my MBE – I needed her advice about what I should wear and we talked about where I could shop for the right outfit. We were just like any two close friends planning a big occasion. Her cancer was a huge elephant in the room. It was as if, by not talking about it, we could kid ourselves that it wasn't actually there.

At the end of my visit, Sonia gave me a list of things she wanted me to get for her. I decided that I would go shopping for lots of glamorous nightwear for her and pampering treats, and we kept our goodbyes upbeat. We looked each other in the eye and silently acknowledged the seriousness of the situation. At that moment, neither of us was prepared to admit to the truth, but I will always remember that look that we shared.

The following day and every day for the next couple of weeks while she was in hospital, I went to see her, always armed with little gifts to try to lift her day. I was determined to make the best of the situation. Her hospital room looked like a shop by the end of her stay there. I think everyone was similarly overcompensating, but it was obviously the only way we could all get through.

Unflappable Sonia, meanwhile, calmly took it all in. She was always an incredibly practical and matter-of-fact person. She asked for a notepad and started making lists. There were people she wanted to see, events she needed to cancel, things in the house she needed to organise and umpteen little jobs she wanted to sort out. She knew that she was on a deadline and, as always, she was determined to get everything done.

The doctors weren't able to say exactly how long she had to live, but, during the two weeks that Sonia was in hospital, the cancer cruelly started to take hold and her handwriting and mobility started to decline. Once all the tests had been completed and it had been confirmed palliative care would be her only treatment, Sonia was allowed to return home to spend the rest of her days with her family.

During this time, I became very close to her children Stephen, Amanda and Jonathan and their spouses Donna, Anthony and

Nicole. Sonia's niece Gabby was also a tower of strength and the star of the catering corps. Many years earlier, Sonia's daughter Amanda and Gabby used to work in my shop, and it was lovely to be reunited with them. I also became very close to Sonia and Alf's grandchildren, who rallied round making lots of cups of tea and filled the house with diverting chatter. There were Friday night suppers together, tea and cakes around Sonia's bedside and lots of stiff-upper-lip behaviour. Of course, there were several occasions where family members were in floods of tears in other rooms of the house, but we tried to stay strong when we were with her.

Sonia, meanwhile, retained her incredible poise and determination, never once succumbing to self-pity. With my investiture coming up, she decided that she wanted to give herself a positive project to work on and would throw a party for me to celebrate my MBE. Bottles of champagne were ordered, canapés were planned and the whole family was invited over to celebrate on the evening of Thursday, 16 February.

CHAPTER 43

After numerous shopping trips, phone calls to seemingly the whole of north London about clothes, etiquette and arrangements, the morning of Thursday, 16 February 2012 finally dawned. It was to be the most memorable day of my life.

After a hurried bit of breakfast – everyone told me that I should eat something before my big day so that I didn't pass out in front of Her Majesty! – I got into the taxi to pick up Mandy, her children and Angela, and then it was off to Buckingham Palace to collect my MBE.

People always say that, on the day you get married, you should try to take in as much as you can as the whole day can race by in a flash, and that's what I tried to do that day. It helps that the event was filmed and I have a DVD of the whole occasion that I can watch back again and again, but on the day I tried my best to drink everything in. And every minute was fabulous.

Once the formalities at Buckingham Palace were over, I was able to relax and the real celebrations kicked off with lunch at the Savoy.

This, of course, was where my beloved Lawrence and I had our wedding reception in 1957, and it seemed fitting to return there that day some 55 years later. After all, he was the reason that my life had been steered the way it had.

As we all enjoyed a glass of champagne together, I raised a glass with Mandy to my lovely Lawrence. We wanted him to be part of the day, too.

After a very long and boozy lunch, I headed off to Sonia's. By this stage, she was very frail. I took my MBE along with me and, bless her heart, she patiently listened as I excitedly recounted every single detail about the day. Then the rest of the family started to arrive and everyone had fun trying on my MBE and pulled my leg about my having a title. It was really very special, the icing on the cake.

The next day, it was back to life as normal for me. I had lots of thank-you letters to write for flowers that I had received and kind messages that had been sent, and of course I went to see Sonia to thank her for arranging my lovely party.

That party was to be the last one Sonia and I shared together. Her health declined quickly over the following few days and, as she started to lose her appetite, the insidious effects of cancer began to take hold. She was in a great deal of discomfort and we all knew she had only a little time left. I tried to make the best of things with her. Her lovely room was gorgeously sunny and faced a beautiful magnolia tree, which was in bloom for the last week of her life, and we would sit quietly and soak up the sun looking into the garden together.

She began to sleep more and more, until there were no words left to say. Tragically, barely a day after she died, her wonderful husband Alf also passed away. His heart was broken and there was simply no way he could live without her. That kind of special love is so beautiful and so rare, and I feel privileged to have been able to call them friends.

I miss Sonia and Alf and the daily phone calls from Sonia asking for news. Alf had always joked that Sonia and I could be together all day and then spend the evening on the phone, too. She was 85 and I was 78, and our friendship had spanned over 40 years.

It was another sad period of my life, but there is always life to live, reasons to keep moving forward and work to be done. And, as if to underline that point, shortly after Sonia and Alf's deaths, I learned that, as part of their legacy, they had left some money for the Alzheimer's Society. Their daughter Amanda asked me to ensure the money would be used effectively on a project that they would really like. Knowing Sonia's enthusiasm for Singing for the Brain, I knew immediately how it would best be used.

I was determined to forge a new relationship between the Alzheimer's Society and Jewish Care, and I started making appointments with people who I thought would be able to help me. It was a matter of getting people from various societies together for meetings to reveal that they shared a common ground as far as dementia and Alzheimer's is concerned. Very soon after our discussions about Singing for the Brain and how it could benefit the community, we were offered the use of a hall in the Otto Schiff home in Golders Green, which is run by Jewish Care. The first session was held on 25 April 2012 and 20 people came along. It was amazing and very emotional for me, as this was what I had hoped for for such a long time.

It wasn't long before I heard from one of the carers who wrote: 'I cannot praise Singing for the Brain enough. I freely admit I was cynical at first, thinking it was childish. I now realise how very, very wrong I was and now see how clever the strategy is behind the sessions. Thank you all so much for this service.'

Soon the word spread, and within a matter of weeks we were full to capacity. It was time to start looking for other venues to expand. With Sonia and Alf's money, I set about trying to secure the second joint venture of the Alzheimer's Society and Jewish Care. This began in February 2013 at Alyth Gardens synagogue in Temple Fortune, north London, and is now in full swing. As we sing the old songs that we all used to love, I can imagine Sonia and Alf laughing and dancing together. I know that they would be so proud.

CHAPTER 44

In March 2013, I went along to a new initiative for the Alzheimer's Society called Dementia Friends. Prime Minister David Cameron, along with the main party leaders, had agreed on a new project to create a million Dementia Friends by 2015. The objective of the project is to spread awareness of dementia and Alzheimer's in the UK, and encourage a greater understanding and acceptance of the condition. With more and more people living longer – and the fact that one in three people over the age of 65 will develop some kind of dementia – it is essential that there is more knowledge of the subject.

The Dementia Friends session that I attended was at the Alzheimer's Society Vice Presidents and Ambassadors lunch in central London and there were about 50 people present. It was so upbeat and designed in such an interesting way. Within 45 minutes, everyone there had grasped the key messages and pledged to spread the word about the cause.

As each new project is rolled out by the Alzheimer's Society, be it

Singing for the Brain or Dementia Friends, I can't help feeling a bit of pride that I was involved in the start of it all. The wonderful thing is that I know there will be more and more incredible initiatives like these, which will continue to make a real difference for people living with Alzheimer's and their carers.

Leaving that Dementia Friends session that day, it struck me that in 2014 I would be turning 80 and the Alzheimer's Society would be celebrating its 35th anniversary, and so it was time for a new project! While my dear friend Sonia was ill, I became close to her daughter-in-law Nicole, who is a journalist. I told her various tales from my past and she suggested that we wrote this book together to help raise some money for the Society – so out came my laptop and off we went!

It has been difficult remembering some of the details of the sad moments in my life. Writing this book, I have come to realise that my coping mechanism has sometimes been to block them out and not think too deeply about the situations as I am living them, be it my cancer when I was a young woman, Lawrence's Alzheimer's or Gerald's cancer. That's just the way I am. If something terrible happens, I just try to get on with it and concentrate on looking forward to the good times.

Throughout my life, I have been lucky enough to go on amazing holidays and, as my 80th birthday was on the horizon, I decided to round off 2013 in style. My friend Helen was also going to be 80 that year, on 19 December, and so we decided to treat ourselves to a cruise in November. We decided it would be lovely to go somewhere that we had never been before – and also somewhere that we were unlikely to go again. We studied all the travel brochures and in the end decided on a cruise that would take us from Barcelona to Rio in Brazil via various ports and then on to Buenos Aires in Argentina.

On 19 November 2013, we flew out to Barcelona, where we had

a whistle-stop tour of our favourite places as we'd both visited the city before. Then the following day we boarded the ship. Our cases – which, needless to say, were packed with a lot more clothes than we were ever likely to need – were hauled on to the ship – I'm so glad we didn't have to carry them! Then we were off on our adventure, two batty 79-year-olds, out to have fun and enjoy ourselves!

The ship stopped at various ports, but it was only when we arrived in Rio de Janeiro that the excursions became really exciting. The ship was there for three days, so we could take our sightseeing at a leisurely pace. Places like Sugar Loaf Mountain, the statue of Christ, Ipanema and Copacabana were all on our tick list, so we couldn't wait to get started. We took a cable car up Sugar Loaf Mountain and had an eye-wateringly expensive lunch in Copacabana, then we had a day to relax before Helen's birthday. On the day, we took a cogwheel train up Corcovado Mountain, and then an elevator followed by an escalator took us up to the Christ statue. The view was absolutely breathtaking and we were very fortunate to have a clear day as the mountain is so often shrouded in clouds.

Helen wanted to go somewhere special for lunch so we went to a restaurant called The Girl From Ipanema, which is where the famous song was written. We had a wonderful meal and Helen felt thoroughly spoiled. She had been in bad health before we went away, so it was fabulous to finally be there, celebrating in the sunshine. We raised our glasses for our departed husbands and made plans for our next 80 years. Well, why not?

We had been told that Rio was the place to buy jewellery, especially gemstones, and I decided that, as it was Mandy's birthday in February, it would be very appropriate for me to buy her an amethyst bracelet. I hoped it was a successful present as it would be a very long way to have to take it back!

The following day, we arrived in beautiful Búzios, which was 'discovered' in the 1960s by Brigitte Bardot and her Brazilian boyfriend. Then, several stops later, we docked in Montevideo, Uruguay, where we thoroughly enjoyed a Jewish Heritage tour. After that, we set sail for Buenos Aires where on our first night we saw the most magical tango show performed on a tiny stage in a beautiful theatre that looked like an old-time music hall.

Our hotel in Argentina was lovely, but we hadn't expected just how hot it was going to be there. It is usually around 29 to 30 degrees, but when we were there it was more like 39 to 40. We were very grateful for air conditioning! Before leaving for London, we had been recommended to book a private tour with a delightful man called Ernesto. He took us around the city and showed us all of the historical sites, including the Metropolitan Cathedral of Buenos Aires, which has the world's only Holocaust memorial that is housed in a cathedral.

I mentioned my interest in Alzheimer's disease and dementia, and asked Ernesto if there were any care homes there. He told me that there was a new home called Ledor Vador and offered to take us there. I was so pleased that I had the opportunity of seeing this wonderful place and was able to meet many of the residents. What stood out in my mind is that they are now creating a centre there for children of one-parent families, the idea being that the children will learn early in life to love and care for the elderly. I found this incredibly inspirational and I started thinking that this is something we could maybe start incorporating in the UK. Because the children and the elderly will be in such close proximity at Ledor Vador, the children will grow up with a much greater understanding of the elderly. This will, of course, mean that dementia and Alzheimer's won't be such difficult subjects for them to grasp.

It was a fabulous trip, and it gave me another idea of how I could help move things forward with dementia and Alzheimer's. I think the idea of giving children a greater understanding of the condition right from the start of their lives could actually start to create a new generation of greater acceptance.

CHAPTER 45

There was one cloud over the holiday, though. Just before I was due to go away on the cruise, I went to see the doctor as I had found I'd been getting short of breath and I kept losing my voice. I thought I must have some kind of virus or a chest infection and I was determined to be 100 per cent fit for the holiday.

Because of my thyroid cancer, the doctor said he wanted to do some tests to rule out that it wasn't anything more serious. The tests came back and, while I was relieved that my cancer wasn't back, I was diagnosed with emphysema – due, no doubt, to the fact that I used to smoke so heavily when I was younger.

Although I had a lovely holiday to look forward to, I also had to face the prospect of living with this horrible lung condition. Having known people with emphysema, I have seen how debilitating it can be with all the shenanigans of having to transport portable oxygen tanks around and so on. But life goes on. From the day I was diagnosed, I decided I would just have to do what I could to stay as well as possible. As soon as the cruise began,

I got a personal trainer to put me through my paces every morning, and I constantly try to keep my brain active. I have always tried to have a positive attitude towards my health.

At the same time, I have realised that, as I approach my ninth decade, my memory is failing to a certain extent; there are many things, for instance, I have forgotten about my childhood and growing up. In the course of writing this book, I have realised my memory isn't what it used to be and this bothers me. But I have to face up to the fact that I am in my 80th year and, much as I would like to be able to remember everything, I know I am fortunate to have plenty of wonderful memories and happy times to celebrate and share. And I'm sure there will be many more to come.

I already have quite a packed diary for the year ahead, and every week there seems to be something in the news about Alzheimer's disease, so there is always more fundraising to be done and awareness to spread. Although I have given up playing golf now – unless I can play to the absolute best of my ability, I don't like playing at all – I am still a social member at my golf club and will continue to help raise money through my annual golf days, bridge evenings and so on. I keep saying that I am too old to continue and that someone else should be in charge, but somehow I am still battling on.

The important thing is to make the most in life. I have so many exciting milestones to look forward to in 2014. After a few unhappy relationships, my darling Mandy met her wonderful Trevor in 2010 and they are due to tie the knot in October 2014. Mandy has always wanted a big family and Trevor has 10 grandchildren, so now she has got it in spades. We also have my grandson Oli's 21st birthday and the 35th anniversary of the Alzheimer's Society to look forward to, so it is going to be a year of big events and happy times.

Over the last few years, I have also learned how to be happy with my own company. When I was younger, I would hate the idea of having days stretched ahead with nothing in the diary and the thought that I would have to be on my own. Now, providing I have a project to work on, I am totally happy by myself. I have finally learned how to relax, enjoy and just 'be'.

No doubt there will be more physical and emotional hurdles to get over in the forthcoming years; there are always testing times for all of us. But no matter what happens, as I have always said, *que sera, sera*. What will be, will be.

AFTERWORD

Jeremy Hughes, CEO of Alzheimer's Society

Mahatma Gandhi's saying 'Be the change you want to see in the world' rings true when I think of the bold and brave decision Morella Kayman made to speak out about her experiences of living with dementia. It was decades ago that she contacted the national press to share her story of caring for her husband Lawrence, who had dementia. It took immense courage for her to speak out in 1972 and take action when dementia was such a taboo. Most people didn't know what the condition was. If they did, they were ashamed or embarrassed to talk openly about dementia and often suffered behind closed doors. It is no exaggeration to say that she was responsible for changing thousands of lives. She began a cycle of openness surrounding dementia and brought together a community of people living with dementia who could support one another. This eventually became what is known today as Alzheimer's Society.

Alzheimer's Society has since grown to become a well-known

charity and organisation that people affected by dementia can turn to for support with over 2,000 services running across England, Wales and Northern Ireland. Services like the Society's Dementia Cafés and Singing for the Brain, which provide an opportunity for people to socialise and get much needed face-to-face support.

It's particularly fitting that we have a National Dementia Helpline too – which answered over 27,000 calls last year. When Lawrence was diagnosed, there was nowhere for Morella to turn and yet instinctively she knew there must be others in a similar situation struggling to cope. This service is now a lifeline for people coping with a diagnosis or caring for a loved one with dementia, with qualified Dementia Advisers signposting people to information and help.

I joined Alzheimer's Society as Chief Executive in 2010, and over the past three years the Society has continued to lead the way in transforming the lives of people affected by dementia. We launched our five-year Strategy, Delivering on Dementia, and have seen our income exceed £70 million for the first time – enabling us to deliver more vital frontline services and fund research into the condition.

Thanks to the campaigning of our staff and volunteers, we've seen vast improvements in the treatments people with dementia receive through the NHS. There was a time when people would automatically be put on harmful anti-psychotic drugs if they showed signs of distress when in reality symptoms could be prevented or managed without medication. We've reached a stage where prescriptions of these dangerous drugs have been reduced by half, and hospitals across the country are learning how to become dementia-friendly in order to better meet the needs of people with the condition.

In 2012, our Prime Minister announced his own challenge on dementia. Giving his voice to the cause and announcing that tackling the condition should be a priority for everyone moved dementia into the spotlight and set the ground for us to take huge strides in caring for people with the condition, funding research and reducing stigma. Then, as part of the Prime Minister's Challenge on Dementia, the G8 Summit in December 2013 was set to focus on dementia research and improvements needed to find the cure.

As the nations gathered in London to make a global action plan on dementia, the reality of how many people dementia affects worldwide came in to sharp focus. New figures revealed a rise in the number of people living with dementia globally – 44 million people now have dementia worldwide, with the total set to soar to 76 million by 2030.

There are currently six times the number of researchers working to find treatments for cancer as there are for dementia. With this huge discrepancy in mind, I went along fired up to ensure we saw the government announce plans for action. Together with charities worldwide, Alzheimer's Society called for leaders from around the world to commit to meaningful, shared steps to drive forward dementia research and agree to a collaborative global action plan. We asked for a significant increase in investment in dementia research. Finally, we looked to the future and how we need to build the field of dementia research, attracting, developing and retaining the best scientists, clinicians and care professionals.

On the day itself, we saw a commitment to double the amount of research funding dedicated to dementia in the UK and a promise of finding a disease modifier or a cure by 2025. While we welcomed these pledges made by government, we recognise how much work is needed to make them a reality. The ambitious task of finding a medical intervention that could change the course of the condition in almost 10 years' time won't come about without a concerted effort from around the world. We recognise the part we have to play as well.

Morella, now a Vice President of Alzheimer's Society, recently said, 'We've still got so much to do and I'm not going to stop now.' A clear testament to the tenacity she has in continuing to support the cause. While I recognise the huge progress that has already been made to improve the reality of living with dementia, I echo her sentiments.

Moving forwards, Alzheimer's Society will continue to push for more on behalf of people with dementia. On 11 December, the day of the G8 Summit, we announced our plan to invest at least £100 million into dementia research, to bring us closer to finding a cure for the future.

Morella has been recognised widely for the inspirational woman she is. She was awarded an MBE in the 2012 New Year Honours list for services to healthcare and more recently a First Women Lifetime Achievement Award for co-founding Alzheimer's Society. Aside from these accolades, I hope Morella sees the very real difference she's made for the thousands of people living with dementia in the UK.

ALZHEIMER'S SOCIETY –
KEY DATES

1979

Cora Phillips SRN, a former dementia carer, hears a radio broadcast by Professor A.N. Davison about research into Alzheimer's disease. She contacts him and, as a result of their discussion, they decide to work together in forming a society concerned with the disease. Professor Gordon Wilcock, Consultant Physician at the Radcliffe Infirmary in Oxford, had previously approached Professor Davison with the same proposal and so Professor Davison introduces Cora and Gordon. Cora also contacts the newly formed American ADS for advice on their Society. Cora and Gordon, together with Dr Anne Hunter and her husband Brian, set up a Steering Committee.

The *Observer* newspaper prints Morella Fisher's story about her husband Lawrence's experience with pre-senile dementia and within days she is flooded with letters from fellow carers. One of the letters, from Cora Phillips, tells Morella about the Alzheimer's group that she has started planning and the two arrange to meet up and discuss a joint venture.

Cora and Morella meet and decide how to move forward with The Alzheimer's Disease Society via fundraising and awareness campaigning. Work begins in earnest to recruit members. Morella agrees to work with Cora, Gordon and Anne on their Steering Committee. The other members of the 1979 Steering Group are Mr Brian Hunter (Solicitor), Mrs Ceri Powell and Mr David Newmark (both carers).

The General Aims of the Steering Committee are agreed: To give support to families by linking through membership. To provide literature to disseminate knowledge of the illness and aids available through social services to cope with it. To see that adequate nursing care is forthcoming in the last bedridden stages. To promote the research and education of the general public and professionals in the understanding of the nature of the illness via the press, media and fundraising.

Following the Steering Group meeting, The Alzheimer's Disease Society is officially established on 6 November. On 17 December 1979, completed charity forms are submitted under the War Charities Act and National Assistance Act 1948, and on 19 December 1979, The Alzheimer's Disease Society becomes a registered charity.

1980

Ninety-eight people attend the first AGM of The Alzheimer's Disease Society. By this time, there are 370 members of the ADS. Twenty area secretaries have also volunteered.

1981

The first newsletter is published for The Alzheimer's Disease Society. A grant from the DHSS is received for the Society's first Development Officer and running costs of a small office. In June, ITV's *World In Action* film a documentary in association with the Society called 'The Quiet Epidemic'. At a two-day symposium in London, it is announced that Alzheimer's disease is no longer linked exclusively with ageing.

1982

Sub-committees are formed for Liaison, Funding, Information, Development, Legal Financial Advice, Finance and Social Work.

1983

A tutor/counsellor is appointed to run the first Alzheimer's counselling course. A Medical Advisory Panel is set up to promote research.

1984

The first Finance Officer is appointed. Abingdon Day Care Centre in Oxford opens.

1985

Manpower Services Commission commences, providing £16,126 a year for staff salaries. A new Day Care Centre opens in Bromley.

1987

Four staff are appointed to work at the Society's new central office in Balham, south London.

1988

The first AGM of Alzheimer's Scotland. A new DHSS grant of £130,000 is made available to people with Alzheimer's.

1990

The Society receives its first legacy.

1991

Cora Phillips is awarded an MBE for founding the Society and for her tireless support to carers.

1994

Membership of The Alzheimer's Disease Society now exceeds 20,000.

1995

Alzheimer's Disease International moves from Chicago to London.

1996

Total income for the Society passes £10 million for the first time.

1998

The Society's website alzheimers.org.uk is launched.

The Society's National Helpline is officially launched by Anne Robinson.

1999

The Alzheimer's Disease Society is renamed Alzheimer's Society.

2000

The first national awareness-raising campaign is launched.

The first Alzheimer's Society Dementia Café in the UK opens its doors in Blackwater Valley.

2001

A 10 per cent year-on-year increase means the Society now has an income of £20 million. The Society becomes the first organisation in the world to have a person with dementia on its board.

2002

Talking Point, the Society's online discussion forum, is launched.

2003

By now, the Society is a £30 million organisation, with over 250 branches across England, Wales and Northern Ireland.

The Singing for the Brain project is first piloted by the then West Berkshire branch of Alzheimer's Society, set up by Chreanne Montgomery-Smith of the branch and Dr Nicholas Bannan (then of the University of Reading). The pilot project is to run for three sessions.

2004

The One Society Programme is launched, a series of changes to infrastructure and working practices.

Following the success of the Singing for the Brain pilot, funding is obtained to run more sessions from January 2004. The project goes on to run successfully until the present day. Its success means the model is implemented in other Society local offices, and adopted as an example of 'best practice' by the Society's Living with Dementia group (Alzheimer's Society's national service user involvement group for people with dementia).

2006

The Dementia Catalogue is launched. This is an online reference database of published materials about all aspects of dementia care and research. At the AGM in September 2006, the society launches its new strategic framework, providing the organisation with a shared set of goals, values and principles.

2007

Alzheimer's Society's seminal Dementia UK report is published outlining the cost and prevalence of dementia in the UK.

Dementia 'Out of the Shadows' report demonstrates the stigma surrounding the condition.

2008

Alzheimer's Society's total income tops £50 million for the first time.

The Society publishes 'Dementia Tax' and 'Home from Home' reports, outlining the cost of social care to people affected by dementia and the need for better-quality care of people with dementia in care homes.

2009

The National Dementia Strategy for England is launched. Personal experiences from members influence the strategy's development.

Alzheimer's Society publishes 'Counting the Cost' report on caring for people with dementia on hospital wards, showing that people with dementia over 65 years of age are using up to a quarter of all hospital beds; 54 per cent of respondents said that being in hospital had a negative effect on the symptoms of dementia.

2010

Launch of 'This is Me' – a simple and practical tool that people with dementia can use to tell staff about their needs, preferences, likes, dislikes and interests in a care home or hospital setting.

February – BBC Dementia Day. Peer-reviewed research is announced showing the benefits of healthy diet and exercise in reducing the risk of dementia.

2011

'Support, Stay, Save' report explores what is needed to help people with dementia to stay living in the community.

A NICE decision in January makes available treatments for Alzheimer's disease accessible to people with the condition.

Tesco becomes Alzheimer's Society's biggest ever corporate partner, raising more than any other Tesco partnership has before, at £7.5 million. As a result of this, the Tesco Dementia Community Roadshow begins touring the UK, offering advice and support to people worried about their memory.

'Short Changed' report on how to protect people with dementia from financial abuse is launched in November.

2012

16 February – Morella Kayman is awarded the MBE for services to Alzheimer's Society on 16 February at Buckingham Palace.

In March, Alzheimer's Society publishes 'Dementia 2012', which sets out evidence on quality of life of people with dementia in England, Wales and Northern Ireland. At the launch of the report,

Prime Minister David Cameron announces The Dementia Challenge – a new initiative to deliver major improvements in dementia care and research by 2015.

Dementia Friendly Communities programme is announced, aiming to encourage towns and communities to proactively include people with dementia in local life and ensure they're supported to remain independent in their communities.

The Dementia Friends programme is announced.

In December, a person with dementia and their carer, Dominic and Jill Batty from Islington, visit 10 Downing Street to meet the Prime Minister with actress Carey Mulligan for the launch of Dementia Friends.

2013
In February, David Cameron becomes a Dementia Friend and invites Alzheimer's Society ambassadors Sally Lindsay, Linda Bellingham and people with the condition to No. 10 to mark the occasion. All three leaders of each political party are now Dementia Friends.

The Society publishes 'Dementia 2013: the hidden voice of loneliness' and 'Building Dementia Friendly Communities: a priority for everyone'. These reports demonstrate the case for investment and development of dementia-friendly communities. A recognition process for communities taking action on becoming dementia-friendly is also launched.

In December, David Cameron names dementia as the focus of G8 and the eight nations meet to discuss ways to collaborate on global

action to tackle dementia. Out of the summit came commitments to:
• find a disease modifier or cure for dementia by 2025;
• double the amount of funding for dementia research; and
• hold Legacy events all over the world in association with OECD, WHO and the European Commission.

At the same time, Alzheimer's Society pledges to raise at least £100 million for dementia research in the next decade.

2014
Alzheimer's Society celebrates its 35th anniversary.

ACKNOWLEDGEMENTS

Writing this book wouldn't have been possible without constant memory-jogging sessions with my daughter Mandy. As always she has been a great help with piecing together details of my life that I had subconsciously filed under 'challenging situations', never to be thought of again.

My sister Angela and my cousins Susi and Martin Goodkind, Peter Goodkind, Barbara Harris and her mother Lily, also Wendy, the wife of Wallace Goodkind. Together they helped me to remember many happy family times.

This has been an ongoing project over the last two years and so I must say a great deal of thanks to Helen and Monica for their contributions.

More thanks go to Vera and Stanley Coleman. I may never have got a diagnosis for Lawrence had it not been for Stanley, and he was the one who helped me write that first letter to the *Observer*. My sincere thanks to his lovely wife Vera for always being there and being a second mum to Mandy whenever necessary.

Eileen Winston, Louisa Sampson and the press office team at Alzheimer's Society have been invaluable in their help supplying information about the history of the Society.

A huge thanks also to Fiona Phillips and Jeremy Hughes for writing such lovely words for the Foreword and Afterword of the book, and to all of the team at John Blake.

There cannot be enough thanks for Nicole, who so willingly said she would be my 'ghost'. She has put so much time and effort into this book, and has become quite passionate about doing whatever she can to help the cause. My thanks also to Jonathan, her husband, for letting her spend so much time on the book, and for so kindly reading and checking it over prior to it being sent to the publishers.